THE FATHER'S FORGIVENESS

The
Father's
FORGIVENESS

rethinking the Sacrament of reconciliation

The Liturgical Press
Collegeville, Minnesota

The Father's FORGIVENESS

rethinking the sacrament of reconciliation

Domiciano Fernández

A Liturgical Press Book

THE LITURGICAL PRESS
Collegeville, Minnesota

Cover design by Greg Becker

Translated from the Spanish, *Dios ama y perdona sin condiciones,* Desclée de Brouwer, Bilbao, Spain, 1989 by Pablo Olmedo cmf

1   2   3   4   5   6   7   8   9

Library of Congress Cataloging-in-Publication Data

Fernández García, Domiciano.
    [Dios ama y perdona sin condiciones. English]
    The Father's forgiveness : re-thinking the sacrament of
reconciliation / Domiciano Fernández ; [translated by Palmo Olmedo].
        p.   cm.
    Translation of: Dios ama y perdona sin condiciones.
    Includes bibliographical references.
    ISBN 0-8146-2087-6
    1. Penance.   2. Reconciliation—Religious aspects—Catholic
Church.   3. Absolution.   4. Catholic Church—Doctrines.   I. Title.
BX2260.F3913   1992
234'.166—dc20   92-7190
                                                     CIP

Contents

Foreword   xi

**Dogmatic Possibility and Pastoral Appropriateness
of the Communitarian Sacramental Absolution
without Private Confession**   1

    Motivation   1

    A Fact of Experience   5

    The Doctrine of the Council of Trent   7

        1. *Obligation of Confession*   9

        2. *General Observations Concerning
            the Texts of the Council of Trent*   15

    The "Pastoral Norms" and their Repercussion   19

    How to Overcome this Difficulty   21

        1. *The Practice of the Early Church*   23

        2. *Theology*   26

    Origins of the Detailed Confession of
    All the Sins   28

    Pastoral Appropriateness   31

**Is there an Obligation to Individually Confess
Grave Sins after Receiving a General
Absolution?**   **35**

Why it Seems that Changing the Legislation
would be Most Correct and Most Reasonable   39

    1. *The Fundamental Question*   39

    2. *With this Understanding there is
Already a More Relevant Answer to
the Question Proposed at the Outset*   41

Penance and Eucharist   **43**

Sacred Scriptures   45

The Ancient Church   46

Council of Trent   52

How is the Question Presented Today?   54

    1. *From the Norms, the Answer is Clear*   54

    2. *This Answer, so Clear from the
Disciplinary Norms is Not
Theologically Satisfactory*   55

    3. *What Does Theology Say?*   58

**Various Sacramental Forms to Celebrate
Conversion**   **63**

Form A: Reconciliation of a Penitent Alone   64

    1. *Unexplored Possibilities of this Rite*   64

    2. *Values of the Private Personal
Reconciliation*   67

Form B: Reconciliation of Several Penitents
with Individual Confession and Absolution   69

Form C: Reconciliation of Many Penitents
with General Confession and Absolution   72

    1. *Norms that at Present Regulate*
        the Celebration of Form C   73

    2. *Present Problems*   76

    3. *Values and Advantages of the*
        Reconciliation of Several Penitents
        with a General Confession and
        a General Absolution   78

    4. *Dangers*   80

Epilogue   85

Glossary

AAS	*Acta Apostolicae Sedis*
CCL	*Corpus Christianorum,* series latina
CSCO	*Corpus Scriptorum Christianorum Orientalium*
ES	*Enchridion Symbolorum,* H. Denzinger, ed.; 32nd ed., A. Schönmetzer, ed. (Freiburg, 1963)
ETL	*Ephemerides Theologicae Lovanienses*
Greg.	*Gregorianum*
LMD	*La Maison-Dieu*
Mansi	J. Mansi *Sacrorum conciliorum nova et amplissimacollectio* (Arnhem and Leipzig, 1927)
NRT	*Nouvelle revue theologique*
RET	*Revista Española de Teología*
Ras. Teol.	*Rassegna di Teologia*
RHE	*Revue d'histoire ecclésiastique*
RSR	*Recherches de sciences religieuses*
Theol. Stud.	*Theological Studies*
Theol. und Philos.	*Theologie und Philosophie*
ZKTh	*Zietschrift für katholische Theologie*

Foreword

This book describes one of many examples where we must return to the Gospel's simplicity and to Christ's example of authentic Christian living. Though people try "to silence the truth" (Rom 1:18) it continues to possess the power to break chains and demolish human barriers and falsehood. Truth nestles in the depths of all human beings, waiting to purify them and enrich them with the fruits of life. "You will know the truth and the truth will make you free" (Jn 8:32). "Your word is truth" (Jn 17:17).

I have pondered long on these inspired words of Paul and John, when reading or explaining the history of the sacrament of penance. At times some people within the Church have tried to imprison God's word, God's grace and forgiveness behind norms, prescriptions, rites and conditions. To a point, structures, mediations and human ways are necessary, but only to a point, for they should never "quench the Spirit of God" (1 Thes 5:19). Such temptation to stifle or quench with all its risks refers not only to bygone days for its persists still: in the synagogue, with the scribes and Pharisees of old; and within people in the Church of our present time. Hence as a guide and norm for our pastoral ministry it seemed necessary to evoke once more the genuine doctrine and again bring to our mind the attitude of Jesus towards sinners.

In the New Testament I have long been impressed by Mark 7 as the strongest and sharpest criticism of the Pharisees' practices and traditions introduced as fulfillment of the Law:

"These people honor me with lip-service, while their hearts stay afar. They worship me in routine observance of human precepts" (Is 29:13).

In other words, in total disregard of God's precept, you cling to human traditions. In Mark, Jesus also told them: "You even put aside the commandment of God to hold fast to your own traditions. Moses said: 'Do your duty to your mother and your father, and if you curse your mother or your father you will be put to death.' But you allow any one to tell a mother or father: 'I can't help you for I have kept all I possess for the Temple.' In this case, you no longer permit your people to help their parents. You nullify the very word of God through the tradition you have handed on. And you do many other things like this as well" (Mk 7:6-13). "You even put aside the very commandment of God in order to implant your own tradition," so that through the tradition you have handed on through generations as an expression of God's will you nullify the word of God.

In essence, they disregarded the Law's ultimate goal, that of authentic worship of God and the service of neighbor. No wonder these words of Jesus must have caused a profoundly shocking impact upon those devout Pharisees, who as zealous observers of the Law were convinced of their own self-righteousness and perfection. But, are the words of Jesus to be viewed merely as a relic of the past? Are they not addressed to us too, to the standards, traditions and practices of today's Church? Let us just recall the bitter history of division between the Oriental and Latin Churches, or that of the Protestant and the Catholic Churches. Were not essentially insignificant issues at times doctored to have decisive importance? At times it has been said that theologians can bestow more importance on a text of the Council of Trent than to the gospel itself or to a genuine teaching of Jesus. Those same theologians can appear more assured of possessing the truth through quoting a certain text of the council — even out of the context — or of some pope, than from reading or meditating on the teachings of the New Testament. Conversely, those persons who open their theological reflections with teachings of the Scriptures as lived and transmitted by the faith of centuries can become a veritable focus of suspicion. It is imperative that we return to Revelation and to its transmission through the Church's history.

To numerous everyday problems of everyone, Jesus has given a clear and sharp answer: "The Sabbath was made for you, not you for the Sabbath" (Mk 2:27). This is a stirring comment from Mark, for the other evangelists seem not to attempt to transcribe this sentence in its original tenor. Perhaps it seemed too strong to them. As E. Käsemann writes: "The community was awestruck at the greatness of the gifts." Perhaps that explains the softer approach of the synoptics: "The Son of Man is Lord of the Sabbath" (Mt 12:8; Lk 6:5; also Mk 2:28). What problems and what oppression could the Church have avoided if this wonderfully pivotal position of Jesus had gained greater impact in Church legislation and in our subsequent attitude and behavior.

In my classes, lectures and continuing formation courses I have dealt with the content of this book at greater depth. At times my students or audience have asked me to put down in writing my conclusions concerning the sacrament of reconciliation, and in particular the integral confession of sins interpreted by the Council of Trent. At first I had certain reservations, convinced that what has to be said has already been said whether in books on history, master's theses or monographs. For more than twenty years I have taught and written on this subject of reconciliation. Now, however, I find it necessary to write a short and simple book in order to reach out to the general reader and also to the priests and bishops, who are usually too caught up in the work of pastoral concerns.

A committee composed of distinguished scholars in the history of penance undertook specific research. The result was a community penitential celebration in which there was general confession and general absolution. In 1972 this was condemned by the Sacred Congregation for the Doctrine of Faith which issued a document on the sacrament of penance denouncing abuses in this respect. I finally resolved to write an article identifying major errors in the principles promulgated since 1972.[1] Primarily I was motivated by the new document of the Spanish Bishops' Conference *Dejaos reconciliar con Dios* (Madrid, 1989) which repeats the same principles, the same norms and prescriptions without any clear awareness of their possible inaccuracy and unacceptability.

My article needed an appendix, which I added together with another one on the presumptive obligation of individually confessing sins earlier forgiven in a celebration with common absolution without individual confession. Finally, I needed a third appendix concerning the importance of the eucharist as a sacrament of reconciliation; a very significant truth not generally recognized in the present Church. I considered it indispensable to add the final chapter on the different forms of penitential celebrations in order to highlight the importance of the private individual confession, whenever sought and desired by the penitent. The private individual confession has existed since the early days of the Church primarily as a form of spiritual direction for monks, even non-priests. Since the seventh century it has been understood as a sacrament, and up to now a highly effective means for the formation of conscience and spiritual growth.

May this book help many to experience again the happiness of reconciliation with God and the Church, for the sacrament of penance is the sacrament of peace and happiness. If we do not regard it in that light, we have the wrong approach. What

---

[1] The first chapter was published in *Revista Agustiniana* 30 (1989) pp. 403-436.

Jesus announced as the good news of reconciliation should, by no means, become a burden, an oppression or a torment. This sacrament can regain its Gospel meaning only if lived as liberation, grace and forgiveness.

CHAPTER 1

Dogmatic Possibility and Pastoral Appropriateness of Communitarian Sacramental Absolution Without Private Confession

MOTIVATION

The Spanish Bishops' Conference has recently published a document on the sacrament of penance.[1] In general it is a thorough document, though lengthy, repetitive and offering nothing new. We should not expect changes in the norms of the ritual of penance, since they must come from the Holy See. The document's focusing on certain questions seems too dependent on the letter of the norms for while it often refers to community penitential celebrations it still insists on the exceptional character of Form C: *reconciliation of several penitents with general confession and absolution*. It was hoped that there would be less of the letter of the law and a more understanding

---

[1] *Dejaos reconciliar con Dios*. Instrucción pastoral sobre el sacramento de la penitencia. Conferencia Episcopal Española, Madrid 1989.

approach towards the well-prepared and communal celebrations, from different settings and in response to specific pastoral needs. However, because changes usually begin at the
grassroots and then eventually are approved by the hierarchy,
such has been the pattern in the long history of the sacrament
of penance. Whenever the norms and canon laws became
outdated, irrelevant, and unresponsive to the people's needs,
new ways of sacramental grace were initiated at the grassroots
level. Within the first six centuries a very significant case of the
Third Council of Toledo in the year 589 takes up this point.

It was commonly held that the sacrament of penance could
be received only once in a lifetime. Because it was considered
as a "second baptism" or a "laborious baptism", and since only
the first baptism was valid, penance was regarded in the same
light. Furthermore, the extremely harsh atonement and satisfaction imposed in the penance deeply affected the penitents'
social and family life (prohibition of marital sexual union or
marriage, prohibition to engage in business or other civil pro-
fessions). The sacrament of penance gradually became a
sacrament of the elderly and of persons who were dying. Some
episcopal synods expressly forbade young persons and mar-
ried couples from receiving penance.[2] From the beginning of
the seventh century the Irish monks went across Europe and
introduced new approaches in the penitential practice, thus
breaking the principle of *irrepeatability* of the sacrament of
penance. The first evidence of this sacrament being received
more than once in a lifetime comes from Spain. In the Council
of 589 convoked by Recaredo, and attended by many bishops
from Spain and France it was noted that some Christians asked
the priest for the sacrament of reconciliation every time they
sinned. And this seemed to the conciliar members an intolerable abuse (*execrabilis praesumptio*). It is valuable here to
recall the words of this great assembly:

---

[2] Cf. Council of Agde (year 506) can. 15; CCL 148, 201; Council of
Orleans (year 538) can. 27; CCL 148A, 124.

"As we were made to understand, in some churches in Spain people do penance for their sins, not in accordance with the canons, but in a reproachable (*foedissime*) way by asking the priest for reconciliation every time they sin. In order to put an end to this execrable presumption (*execrabilis praesumptio*), this holy council establishes that penance be administered according to the canonical form of the early faithful. That is, those who repent from their sins are to be suspended first of all from communion and be submitted to the imposition of hands together with the rest of the penitents. After the time of satisfaction may they be accepted back to communion according to the opportunity established by the priest. Those who, whether during the penance or after the reconciliation fall into their previous sins, are to be excommunicated in accordance with the norms of the old severity of the canons."[3]

Despite the opposition of the hierarchy, this new form found almost immediate acceptance. Half a century afterwards a synod in France accepted and even recommended granting the "penance" to the faithful, provided they have confessed.[4] Today we face a similar situation, for since the Second Vatican Council new forms of celebrating the sacrament have surfaced among priests and faithful. Again it has been the hierarchical Church which has opposed and disapproved some of these celebrations born at the grassroots level.

The *Pastoral Instruction* of the bishops stresses the need for an individual confession and struggles to find a reasonable explanation to an anomalous norm: *the obligation to confess the mortal sins after having received absolution without previous individual confession.* This particular point is not well established and consequently the issue is difficult to resolve. The whole problem derives from a false understanding of an

---

[3]Can. 11; Mansi VI, 708.
[4]Synod of Chalon-sur-Saône around 650, can. 8; CCL 148A, 304.

important canon of the Council of Trent. Unfortunately this error has been repeated in later documents. As formulated in the new Code, this principle states:

"Individual and integral confession and absolution constitute the sole ordinary means by which a member of the faithful who is conscious of grave sin is reconciled with God and with the Church. Physical or moral impossibility alone excuse that person from such confession, in which case reconciliation may be gained by other means also" (Canon 960).

In the light of history and later theology, this principle is quite wrong as this explanation will demonstrate. It has been the focus of innumerable discussions during the preparation of the New Ritual of Penance and in 1972 it provoked a stern reaction from Cardinal Seper. Before the publication of the new *Ordo penitentiae* which was then being prepared, he promulgated a document of the Congregation for the Doctrine of the Faith *Sacramentum paenitentiae*.[5] This interpretation seriously hindered a deeper renewal within the Church, as the following brief explanation testifies.

Immediately after the Council on December 2, 1966, competent theologians formed a committee for the renewal of the sacrament of penance,[6] so that by 1968 the publication of the new *Ordo* was already anticipated. Unfortunately several events within the Church blocked its progress. There was a reorganization of the Roman congregations; the Council for the Appli-

---

[5] *Normae pastorales circa absolutionem sacramentalem generali modo impartiendam*, whose first words are "Sacramentum paenitentiae," AAS, (1972) 510-514.

[6] The first commission was composed of J. Lécuyer (president), F. Heggen (secretary; when F. Heggen retired, F. Nicolasch became the secretary), Z. Alszeghy, P. Anciaux, C. Floristán, A. Kirchgässmer, L. Ligier, K. Rahner, C. Vogel. All of them are noted authors of significant studies on penance, like C. Vogel, P. Anciaux, K. Rahner, J. Ligier, etc.

cation of the Constitution on Liturgy and the Congregation of Rites were dissolved and then reformed as the Congregation for Divine Worship; and finally the committee for the sacrament of penance was also changed.[7]

On the other hand, before the new norms were yet published some priests introduced community penitential celebrations including a general confession or some other sign of repentance followed by general absolution. There was no previous individual confession included. This introduction alarmed the prefect of the Congregation for the Doctrine of the Faith. In an attempt to cut off what he considered to be intolerable abuses, he published the aforesaid document with the aim of clarifying doctrines and proposing the norms which should regulate such community celebrations. Most of these norms have since been adopted in the new Ritual of Penance. To their discredit, they have impeded and still do impede Form C from becoming the *ordinary way*, as designed by the first committee (that is reconciliation of several penitents with general confession and common absolution). This development has continued to have serious consequences for many of the faithful who could otherwise receive sacramental forgiveness but now do not receive it in any form. For this reason it is necessary to confront this issue objectively and rationally.

A FACT OF EXPERIENCE

It is widely known that when a penitential celebration with sacramental absolution without previous individual confession is announced, a large congregation receives the sacrament. It has been noted that with the benign interpretation of the bishop, the faithful from different parishes and neighboring villages would

---

[7] The second commission was composed of P. Jounel (president), F. Sottocornola (secretary), J.A. Garcia, P. Visentin, H. Meyer, K. Donovan, G. Pasqualetti.

participate in such celebrations held in other parishes or in different dioceses. This is to be interpreted as a good sign, and not as an abuse. It is a trend which the hierarchical Church should accept in the light of the Gospel and examine whether these changes come from the Holy Spirit. In the history of penance such a course of events has not been unknown.

The point is not to make the forgiveness of sins easy or difficult, but to reconcile persons with God, with the Church and with one another, in order to facilitate a sincere conversion. The aim is to help the faithful experience happiness in God's forgiveness and to assist them towards a more authentic and committed Christian life. If such an aim is better achieved with community celebrations than with individual confession, then there is no valid reason to forbid them. The dogmatic difficulties can be overcome, as proved by findings of the specialists in the sacrament of penance. This form of communal reconciliation should not be lightly discarded. "The expression 'easier way' or 'more difficult way' is close to considering individual confession as a punishment; and such would not be the proper approach to the sacrament of penance."[8] The crisis of sacramental penance, referred to in the *Introduction to the Pastoral Instruction,* has deeper roots. It will not be solved by suppressing individual confession and promoting community celebrations. In order to celebrate worthily it is necessary to live a sincere Christian life and experience personal conversion. If we are committed, however, we must acknowledge regrettably that what nowadays distances many faithful from receiving the sacrament of penance is precisely the obligation to confess to a priest all their grave sins. For many persons, individual confession is necessary and they find in it the peace and joy of being forgiven, while for others it is a torment. If God does not demand it, to impose on all the obligation of confession is a grave burden.

---

[8] J. IMBACH: *Perdónanos nuestras deudas,* Santander 1983, p. 177.

THE DOCTRINE OF THE COUNCIL OF TRENT

For some theologians, and in particular for the Roman congregations, the major difficulty in admitting Form C of general confession and absolution as the ordinary form of reconciliation derives from the teachings of the Council of Trent. The texts of Trent are clear enough, but they are to be approached and interpreted within their own historical context as countering the doctrine of the Reformers. Some frequently used sentences should be taken into account like "iure divino" (of divine right), "heresy", "be anathema", etc.[9] It is interesting to note that Martin Luther and John Calvin do not reject private confession of sins, but rather its obligation and its being a sacrament instituted by Jesus Christ. Luther used to confess his sins; and he affirms that he would not allow this practice to be snatched away for any reason, as his words testify:

> "I do not want to be deprived of the secret confession by anybody, and I would not leave it for any earthly treasure for I know how much strength and consolation it has given me. Nobody knows about the power of private confession, because we have often to fight and struggle against the devil. I would have been overcome and strangled long ago had I not kept the practice of confession... See therefore

---

[9] There are many articles on the meaning of these expressions in the Council of Trent. Let us quote some: P. FRANSEN: *Réflexions sur l'anathème au concile du Trente*, ETL 29 (1953) 657-672; A. MARRANZINI: *Valore del' "anathema sit" nei canoni tridentini*, Ras. Teol. 9 (1963) 27-33; H. VORGRIMLER: *Das Bußakrament iuris divini?*, Diakonía 4/5 (1969) 257-266; K. RAHNER: *Reflection on the concept of "ius divinum" in Catholic thought, Theological Investigation* V, 219-243; K.J. BECKER: *Die Notwendigkeit des vollständigen Bekenntnisses in der Beichte nach dem Konzil von Trient*, Theol. und Philos. 47 (1972); A. AMATO: *I pronunciamenti tridentini sulla necessitá della confesione sacramentaria nei canoni 6-9 della sessione XIV (25 novembre 1551)*, Las-Roma, 1974; M. NICOLAU: *"Jus divinum"* on the confession in the Council of Trent, RET. 32 (1972) 419.439; CARL J. PETER: *Dimensions of Jus divinum in Roman Catholic Theology*, Theol. Stud. 34 (1973) 227-250.

that private confession is not despised, for it is a very valuable practice which I myself do not want to dissuade anyone from for anything in the world."[10]

Even so, such a eulogy on voluntary private confession does not restrain Luther from strongly rejecting it as a papal imposition and as involving the obligation to confess all one's sins. Instead of a relief and consolation, this would be a torment and a torture for a person.[11]

Canon 7 of the Council of Trent is highly significant in decisively influencing the *Pastoral Norms* published in 1972, subsequent documents and even the new Code of Canon Law. In full, it states:

"If anyone said that for the remission of sins in the sacrament of penance it is not necessary by divine right to confess each and every one of the mortal sins that can be recalled after a suitable and a serious examination; (nor is it necessary for) even the hidden sins and those ones against the two last commandments of the decalogue and the circumstances that change the species of sin, but said that confession is useful only to instruct and to console the penitent; and that in the olden times it was observed only to impose canonical satisfaction; or if anyone said that those who make an effort to confess all their sins do not want to leave; or if anyone said that it is not licit to confess all the venial sins, let him be anathema" (DS 170; Collantes 1177).

This, of course, is not the only text in the Council of Trent which refers to the obligation to accuse oneself of one's sins.[12] There

---

[10] Edit. Weimar, 10, 3, 61-64.
[11] Weimar, 2, 645, 16; Weimar 8a, 58, 5.
[12] See chapters 8 and 9 (DS 1708 and 1709); chapter 5 (DS 1679-1680) etc.

are other documents that demand the confession of sins to a priest.[13] In the Latin Church, with varying degrees of emphasis since the Middle Ages, the accusation of one's self of all sins has been demanded.[14] With regard to the texts of the Council of Trent, it is not necessary to again return to their interpretation for much has already been written. Besides, the difficulty does not lie within the contents of the text, but in rather determining for today the obligation and value of a norm given within circumstances vastly different from our own. This particular focal point is the subject of this present study.

Obligation of Confession

In addressing the entire chapter V on confession (DS 1679-1683) and the corresponding canons (cc. 6-8; DS 1706-1707) the Council of Trent clearly believed that confession of all sins to a priest was a divine precept and hence obligatory, unless some grave causes, physical or moral, would excuse a person from this obligation.

It is also necessary to understand that this complete confession of all grave sins was understood as the "human mode", that is, within the limits and deficiencies of human nature. Because God does not demand the impossible, many are the pronouncements by which the council tries to soften and humanize this obligatory declaration of all the sins, those sins

---

[13] Before Trent, Pope Martin V demanded the integral declaration of sins from the followers of Hus and of Wycliff (DS 1260); in the Council of Florence this doctrine is included in the decree "Pro Armenis" in 1439 (DS 1325).

[14] See the book by J. ESCUDÉ: *La doctrina de la confesión íntegra desde el concilio de Letrán hasta el concilio de Trento*, Barcelona, 1967; J.E. LOZANO ZAFRA: *La integridad de la confesión, ¿Precepto positivo divino o norma eclesiástica?* Roma 1977; J.A. DO COUTO: *De integritate confessionis apud patres concilii tridentini*, Romae 1963; D. FERNÁNDEZ: *El sacramento de la reconciliación*, Edicep, Valencia 1977, pp. 259-275; *XXX Semana Española de Teología: El sacramento de la penitencia*, C.S.I.C., Madrid 1972 with diverse studies on the confession of sins in the Council of Trent.

which could be remembered only after a diligent examination. The council does not aim at tormenting the conscience of the faithful, but at developing in them a duty to be considered as sacred. It is evident that this is a formal and not *material* integrity. The council also refers to the *secret* confession; and some Fathers even wanted the secret confession to a priest only to be defined as *de iure divino*. Fortunately this proposition was not accepted. For the Council of Trent, while the confession of sins was necessary, the *mode* of confessing, whether private or public, was a human right. Public confession was neither commanded nor prohibited by Christ (DS 1683). In order to oppose the doctrine of the Reformers, the Fathers insisted far too much on the obligation of confessing sins.

There is no valid motive in denying that such affirmation of Trent seems to be inaccurate or false. In order to give an explanation in line with the present historical context, it is possible for a hermeneutic of the texts to deny the dogmatic value of these propositions or simply to affirm that they are no longer obligatory. It is blatantly dishonest to deny that such affirmation was made, or to distort its meaning by any subtle and arbitrary interpretation. From this open approach of honestly admitting what is already written, I can in no way hide my surprise and admiration whenever I read these and other texts in the light of the *Scriptures* and of the *penitential practice of the early Church*. In several places they accord neither with Scripture nor with history.

Scripture

In order to prove this "divine precept" of confessing all sins, scriptural proof is weak and therefore quite unconvincing. Moreover the stated norms do not conform with Jesus' behavior. The biblical texts quoted in support of the divine precept are Mt 16:19, 18:18; Jn 20:23; Lk 17:14; James 5:16; 1 Jn 1:9.

The texts of Mt 16:19 (words addressed to Peter) and 18:18 (words addressed to the disciples) specifically refer to the power to *bind* and *unbind*. As such, they do not refer exactly to the sacrament of penance, but to a more general power which prohibits or permits the power of declaring something licit or prohibited, either to expel someone from the community or readmit someone to the community. Such an interpretation is not specific and therefore it may also apply to the forgiveness of sins. Since they referred to this power as the sacrament of penance, the Fathers of Trent argued that knowledge of the particular sins is required in order to be able to *bind* or *unbind*.

This interpretation also holds for the text of Jn 20:23, which the Council of Trent understood as the institutional text of the sacrament of penance: "for those whose sins you forgive, they are forgiven; for those whose sins you retain, they are retained." In the Gospels this text is clearly the most explicit text concerning the power given to the apostles to forgive sins. As in the texts of Matthew, to *forgive* or to *retain* demands some knowledge of the person for whom forgiveness is granted or denied. Just to demand a certain declaration or confession of sins, we should not minimize the force of this argument. It is seriously inaccurate to deduce from this any precept of the Lord binding on all to declare all serious sins, even the hidden ones, in order to obtain forgiveness. In no way do the biblical texts go as far as this.

The text of James 5:16 here offers a significant statement: "There will be healing if you confess your sins to one another and pray for each other." The whole context suggests sickness, blessing, prayer for the sick, forgiveness of sins and healing. In the Middle Ages when the priest was absent, this was the classic text used to justify the hearing of confession by lay people. Nowadays this text is generally considered as the main biblical source for the blessing of the sick.

Addressed as it is to all Christians, can this exhortation really be interpreted as a precept binding all the faithful to declare all sins to a priest? Moreover, it does not seem that these words apply to the earlier institution of the sacrament of penance.

The first letter of John specifically mentions recognizing and confessing our sins before God, not before a priest: "If we confess our sins, he, who is faithful and just, will forgive us our sins and cleanse us from all wickedness" (1 Jn 1:9). Even less does Christ's order to the lepers refer to the sacrament of penance and the forgiveness of sins: "Go and show yourselves to the priests" (Lk 17:14). This is merely a legal requirement in order to regain social status within the society. From such a biblical basis, it is difficult to refer to any divine precept binding persons to confess to a confessor all serious and hidden sins in order to obtain God's forgiveness.

Judicial character of the sacrament of penance

To urge the detailed confession of sins, the judicial character of the sacrament is generally used. This is referred to as the tribunal of penance, for the priest is regarded as a judge and a doctor. He must really know therefore the offender or the sick person. The conciliar text itself presents the priests in this ministry of forgiveness as *praesides et iudices* (DS 1679), as presidents and judges. When the text refers to absolution, it warns that the priest cannot limit himself to the mere proclamation of the Gospel or to declare to the penitent that God has forgiven the sins. Rather, absolution is seen as administered by a judicial act (*ad instar actus iudicialis*) in which the sentence is pronounced by the priest presiding as judge (*velut a iudice*) (DS 1685).

The Council of Trent clearly establishes a comparison but in no way fully equates the act of absolution with the act of a civil power, or the absolution by the priest as a function of a civil judge. It needs to be remembered that the original text refers to a "truly judicial act" and the adverb *"ad instar"* — *by way of* — replaces *vere*. The council seeks to emphasize the efficacy of an absolution which does not consist in being merely pronounced: God has already forgiven you.

In this consideration we cannot deny that the function of the priest is certainly similar to that of the judge who examines a lawsuit and forgives or condemns, and to that of the person who grants something, with some attached obligation. But this is by way of analogy and not by direct equation. For the detailed and prescriptive confession of all sins, the arguments deduced from the *judicial character* of the sacrament of penance therefore do not possess all the force that some would like. Such a route diverges far from the reality of both the spirit and the letter of the Council of Trent. This is because in those years the bipartite division of *administrative power* and *judicial power* as such did not exist. Consequently the judicial power dealt with not so much the concession of an indult or grace as with either the condemnation or absolution of an accused. The Council of Trent understood this as *alieni beneficii dispensatio* (DS 1685). Following Trent's words present-day theologians who would like to deduce the exact knowledge and details of the cause in order to give a just sentence base themselves on the present juridical order and terminology. Consequently, they distance themselves from the teaching of the Council of Trent. Considering the present division of powers, the act of absolution resembles an act of the graceful administrative power, rather than that of a judicial process in the modern sense.[15] Elsewhere this subject has already been dealt with at length, so it serves little purpose to elaborate further since it is easy to refer to works of recent authors.

Confession is necessary *iure divino*

There is yet another point which deserves close attention and reflection. The Council of Trent and subsequent documents deriving from it affirm that confession to a priest of all grave sins is of *iure divino* (cf. DS 1679; 1706; 1707). Nowadays no one can deny that this expression has a broad meaning in the texts of Trent. As long ago as 1547, one of the theologians of Trent explained the meanings of this expression as:

---

[15] Cf. F. GIL DE LAS HERAS: *Carácter judicial de la absolución sacramental según el concilio de Trento*, Burgense 3 (1962) 151-153.

1. what is included in the Sacred Scriptures, in the Old and the New Testaments;
2. what is implicitly included in the Scriptures and is deduced from it as a necessary consequence;
3. statutes of the councils of the Church. This decree can also be called a "human right",[16] that is, it can derive from a prescription that proceeds from God, or Christ, or from the customs of the Church.

What really is of concern is knowing the sense of the expression "of divine right" in this chapter V on penance and its respective canons. The easiest response is to regard its use in the full sense, but to the Council of Trent integral confession of sins was necessary "by divine right" in the first sense. That is, it is a precept of the Lord, or expressly revealed, since it is affirmed that the sacrament was instituted by the Lord (DS 1679). This interpretation is founded on the biblical texts mentioned earlier: James 5:16; 1 Jn 1:9; Lk 17:14. This is not to assert that the Council of Trent was correct or that this is an infallible truth. The biblical texts do not prove this and later history is opposed to such an affirmation. Canon 6, for instance, declares that from the beginning the Church has always practiced secret confession to a priest only. This, however, does not correspond to reality (cf. DS 1706). If we were to admit that all affirmations of all councils are infallible and unchangeable, then in theology we could take no further steps forward. It should be no surprise that conciliar Fathers speak from the historical knowledge of their own time and read the Scriptures with the mentality of their own era. Nowadays well-founded historical and exegetical findings demand that we revise certain earlier conclusions.

---

[16] *Fr. Antonio Delfino.* Cf. CT, edic. Görres, 6, 1.70.

Sign of true contrition

In several separate places, the conciliar texts identify further reasons for prescribing the individual confession of sins. True conversion tends to be seen as manifest and centered in the acts of confession and satisfaction. Those who refuse any humble confession of sins show that they are not truly repentant. The sincere confession of sins is a necessary or natural consequence of a sincere conversion. We agree. But let us not forget that the confession of sins is not the only gesture that outwardly expresses sincere conversion. The ancient texts barely mention confession and they refer repeatedly to tears, fasts, prostrations, hairshirt and ashes. These represent valid alternatives to the actual confession of sins.[17]

General Observations Concerning Texts of the Council of Trent

1. The council Fathers regarded private individual confession as the historically established norm for administering the sacrament of penance, which in fact does not correspond to historical reality. The Fathers did not totally ignore other public forms of penitential celebrations within the early Church but did not overly concern themselves with these forms. Their major concern focused on the Reformers' rejection of the necessity of the private confession of sins as the then ordinary mode of receiving the sacrament of priestly absolution.

---

[17] See a number of texts in the book by C. VOGEL: *El pecador y la penitencia en la Iglesia antigua,* Barcelona 1968. We indicate some: *Didascalia,* chapter 2, numbers 10-13 (Vogel, p. 107); TERTULLIAN, *De paenitentia,* chapter 9 (Vogel, pp. 144-145); CYPRIAN, *De Lapsis,* chapter 16 (Vogel, pp. 125-126); ST. AUGUSTINE, *Sermo 52* (Vogel, p. 171); JOHN CASSIAN, *Collatio XX* (Vogel, p. 181); ST. CAESARIUS OF ARLES, *Sermo 64, 4* (Vogel, p. 231). Allusion to shame for the confession of sins is rare. The fact itself of undertaking public penance was a manifestation of their condition as sinners. St. Caesarius of Arles says: "Let anyone who is not ashamed to commit sins that are to be atoned for through penance, not be ashamed either to do it" (Sermo 65; PL 39.2223; Cf. Vogel, p. 231).

2.   It is an anomaly to apply to the community celebrations the same norms that the Council of Trent established for private individual confession. Nor is it proper to resort to the texts of the past, with their different historical context, in order to resolve the present-day problems. These have sprung specifically from the vain attempt to revitalize and renew the administering of a sacrament that has been relegated to a totally unsatisfactory and private practice.

3.   It is evident that the texts of Trent, if they are still valuable, can be applied only to a private individual celebration. They cannot apply to the community penitential celebrations, which constitute a distinctly different mode of celebration. The question remains that if during the course of the history of penance there have been such radical changes in its form, why today can we not accept a change in an aspect which is secondary? While I may admit the divine right in the obligation to confess all grave sins in the reconciliation of only one penitent, even so, I see no difficulty for the institutional Church in authorizing other modes of celebration with only general confession. These constitute merely diverse forms of celebrating the sacrament. That such a basic attitudinal change to them is possible is amply demonstrated from history.

4.   The obligation to confess all one's sins has never been considered as an *absolute* obligation, but only a conditional one. This conclusion is demonstrated by the numerous circumstances and situations in which it is possible to omit complete confession, namely, in the case of the dying, the deaf and the dumb, ignorance of language, the large number of penitents and the lack of priests, etc.[18]

---

[18] Cf. D. FERNÁNDEZ, *El sacramento de la reconciliación,* pp. 262ff, where we present the main causes for dispensation and the historical facts in which the Holy See has granted this dispensation from the accusation of sins. Some more cases are presented in the multicopied document of the *"Coetus XXIII bis, Schemata 279, De paenitentia 6"* of March 16, 1968 of the "Consilium ad exsequendam Constitutionem de Sacra Liturgia," pp. 38ff.

5. Since many of the faithful who confess frequently or participate in penitential celebrations wrongly consider certain acts to be mortal sins, there is one further fact to consider. In essence, such acts do not sever the relationship of love and communion with God, nor are they seen to destroy the fundamental option to serve God and neighbor. Since there is no obligation to confess the non-grave sins, a general absolution could be administered in a community celebration without contravening in any way the ordinance of the Council of Trent. Such is the approach of Fr. Z. Alszeghy in an article written long before the publication of the New Ritual of Penance.[19]

Fr. Alszeghy puts this question openly: *Can the hierarchy introduce the practice of the congregational sacramental absolution which overlooks the private declaration of sins?* His answer is taxative: Trent has defined the necessity of submitting to the priest all mortal sins. Only a physical or moral impossibility can dispense a person from individual confession.[20] In his article the strictness of this answer is mollified by a series of cases or circumstances which permit the community absolution.[21]

The major differences between my view and that of Fr. Alszeghy is that he places too much stress on the texts of the Council of Trent and he attempts to extend their normative value within the present circumstances. For my part, more attention should be given to the real problems a deficient penitential praxis presents today and then a solution sought in the light of the Gospel and the whole of the Church's tradition. Clearly, the Council of Trent does not represent the whole of the Church's tradition.

---

[19] Z. ALSZEGHY: *Problemi dogmatici della celebrazione penitenziale comunitaria*, Greg 48 (1967) 577-587. We have discussed in length about this and its position in our article, *Renovación del sacramento de la penitencia, Nuevas perspectivas*, Pastoral Misionera, Sept.-Oct. 1967, number 5, pp. 54-71.

[20] Z. ALSZEGHY, Ibid., pages 580-581. We summarize the author's view.

[21] Ibid., p. 584.

6.   With this, we raise a much wider and much more pertinent problem, which we cannot treat here. Sometimes we become lost in the texts without examining their underlying reality. That we become preoccupied with the letter, and therefore we tend to neglect the spirit, can be called a "pharisaic" attitude. A genuine inner conversion through the Church's mediation is essential for the forgiveness of sins and the regaining of God's grace and friendship. True repentance is manifested in many ways and not only through the confession of sins. By themselves tears have long been a more eloquent and more sincere language than words. At times, a closer knowledge of the penitent can be better obtained through a gesture or a few words than through the detailed telling of sins. There is a special case for persons who can willingly and freely approach a priest and can kneel down and say: "Forgive me, Father, because I have sinned many times," and then burst into tears. Such persons have fulfilled all requirements and therefore should be given words of encouragement, and then absolution. There is no need at all to demand any accurate and detailed confession of sins. As priests, I believe we have all experienced something of this nature.

Essentially, we should never become slaves of the letter and its norms. Rather we should help penitents to find happiness and forgiveness and bring them to the trusting assurance that God loves and forgives them. The surest proof of a sincere repentance is a change for the good in one's way of life. In the early Church the community waited for this effective change before granting any reconciliation. Nowadays no one would be surprised to hear the pope himself or any preacher proclaim that the best penance is the change in one's way of life. I believe this doctrine is well known. Luther preached this doctrine in a sermon on penance, but this proposition was soundly condemned by Leo X: *Optima paenitentia, nova vita* (DS 1457). While we need to consider the entire historical context, we are forced to conclude that such condemnation of this doctrine remains surprising and painful.

7. With regard to the actual forgiveness of sins, I believe that we need to reflect more on the historical origins and on the true meaning of the integral confession. In the present era, the question that continually confronts us is why the confessing of sins has been so strictly demanded, and the overall purpose of confession so sadly overlooked. In the overall understanding of the sacrament of penance persons query the essential role of the confession of sins and the different forms of accusation. Questions also surround the relationship between the integrity of confession and the other values or demands of the authentic conversion of the Christian sinner.

The historical origins are sufficiently clear, but in no way should they be overlooked. The return to those origins, to the Gospel texts and to giving to God the primary responsibility in the work of reconciliation can thus shed light on some aspects that for some persons still seem obscure.

THE "PASTORAL NORMS" AND THEIR REPERCUSSION

With regard to the recent documents of the Holy See with Cardinal F. Seper as its prefect and Monsignor P. Philippe as its secretary, the 1972 *Pastoral Norms* of the Congregation for the Doctrine of the Faith have carried far more weight than has the Council of Trent itself. The interpretation proposed by the 1972 Pastoral Norms was adopted almost entirely by the Penitential Rite (nos. 31-34) and the new Code of Canon Law (canons 960-963), which in some cases is even more prescriptive, contains its essence.

Canon 960 opens by repeating what is affirmed in norm I: *individual and private confession and absolution constitute the only ordinary means of reconciliation.* This is followed by a statement concerning the essential norms that regulate the general absolution of those penitents who have not previously confessed as individuals (c. 961). For penitents to receive validly general sacramental absolution it is necessary:

1. that the penitents be duly prepared;

2. that penitents have the intention, in due time, to make their individual confession of all grave sins not yet confessed (c. 962);

3. that the individual confession must be made as soon as possible, and before receiving another general absolution (c. 963).

While the first requirement seems obvious, the second one established by canon 962 is questionable. This canon affirms not only the obligation of the faithful to declare all their grave sins not yet confessed; it also establishes as a requirement for the validity of the sacramental absolution that persons are to have this intention. Basically, I believe that God's ways are quite distinct from the canonical prescriptions. If the faithful truly repent by receiving sacramental absolution they are genuinely reconciled with God and with the Church. The added prescription of a later individual confession of grave sins not yet confessed is a church law and as such it does not affect God's forgiveness.

The scholastics affirmed that all acts of true contrition implicitly carry the *votum sacramenti.* In so affirming they tried to explain that an act of perfect contrition wipes away sins. Now, although the case appears to be the same, it is in fact quite different. Added is the requirement that for the validity of the sacraments, penitents need to be ready to confess privately to a minister all grave sins not yet confessed. The solution to this problem is difficult:

a. If the precept to confess individually all grave sins is identified with God's will, then there can be no true conversion nor true repentance if persons are not ready to fulfill God's will.

b. But for those who do not identify with a divine precept the obligation to declare all grave sins to the confessor, they can still have true repentance for having offended

God and the community or society. They can still receive forgiveness and the sacramental grace without having the intention of afterwards accusing themselves privately of all non-confessed grave sins. Such is my judgment, but needless to say, it is not easy to determine now just which sins can be considered grave. In the early Church there were earnest attempts to reduce them to three, in order to satisfy the ecclesiastical penance. If there are only two categories of sins: firstly, *mortal* or *grave,* and secondly, *venial* or *light,* it is indeed difficult to impose as God's will the confession of all grave sins. It is quite a different situation to show some external sign of repentance in order to gain the grace of the sacrament.

HOW TO OVERCOME THIS DIFFICULTY

With regard to the reconciliation of several penitents without any previous individual confession we have stated at the outset that, for many, the main difficulty stems from the teachings of the Council of Trent. Although urging the obligation of confession more than Trent itself, the other documents do not possess nearly the same dogmatic impact. One simple method of solving this difficulty is to classify it as merely a *disciplinary norm* and not a dogmatic affirmation. By this means those who fear to transgress any teaching of an ecumenical council will be free from scruples. A number of canons from the Council of Trent and other councils have been abandoned without causing any subsequent problems. The first ecumenical Council of Nicea (325) prohibits persons from praying on their knees on Sundays or on the feast of Pentecost by ordering them to pray in a standing position.[22] It prescribes the re-baptizing and re-

---

[22] Can. 20; *Concil. Oecum. Decreta*, edit. Alberigo, Herder, Freiburg 1962, p. 15.

ordaining of those Paulinians who returned to the Catholic Church.[23] The Lateran Council IV, that one which prescribes the annual confession and communion also prescribes that all Christians distinguish themselves from Jews and Saracens[24] by their manner of dress. The Council of Trent condemns those who affirm that the Mass should be celebrated only in the language of the people, and those who affirm that water should not be mixed with the wine to be offered.[25] It needs to be constantly reinforced that from a historical perspective, the prescriptions of any council are largely conditioned, and even determined, by the prevailing customs and mind set of that era. Consequently, across time and cultures in line with this approach such prescriptions cannot be applied indiscriminately.

A sound and basic hermeneutic prohibits any scholar from setting an absolute and unconditional value on the early Church texts. For example the Council of Trent demands the confession of all sins for their forgiveness. Besides opposing the Protestant doctrine, this teaching means that the rightful administration of the sacrament demands the knowledge of the penitent's state. To be able to retain or to forgive, in general terms it is necessary to possess the knowledge of what is retained or forgiven. It cannot be deduced from here, however, that the detailed confession of all sins is necessary. Sinners and their attitudes matter far more than the sins. No one doubts that for this it is necessary that penitents somehow manifest their sorrow, recognizing themselves as sinners who are asking for forgiveness. This requirement, however, can be manifested in diverse ways. In the early Church for example, placing oneself in the "order of penitents" implied already a confession of sins; this applied, at least, to the most serious ones. Thus, although the sins are not specified or listed, the participation in a penitential celebration is already a sign of one's acknowledg-

---

[23] Canon 19; Ibid., p. 14.
[24] Const. 68; Ibid., p. 242.
[25] Sess. XXII, can. 9; DS 1759.

ment of being a sinner. In these circumstances a general confession could be even more recommended and more liberating than any detailed confession of sin.

It is only by re-examining earlier related history and its associated theology that we can hope to solve those difficulties presented by the Council of Trent, and those presented by the teachings of the Church's magisterium.

The Practice of the Early Church

If we explore the history of ecclesiastical penance in the first centuries it is difficult to conclude that sins are forgiven only by the integral confession of the penitent and absolution by the priest. For several centuries the only sacramental penance in the Church was not understood as an ordinary means, but rather as something extraordinary, rare, exceptional, and granted only once in a lifetime. In those times, no doubt, persons sinned more than once before and after having received the sacrament of penance. This presented a problem to only a few, because "practically, at least since the fifth century, *most Christians* could receive the official sacramental reconciliation only when they were about to die."[26] Even in these circumstances, a complete confession of sins was not usually demanded. This is not to say that those persons were exempted from the integral confession, because such a precept was non-existent. Officially, it was sufficient that the persons manifest the motives and causes that moved them to ask for reconciliation. Let us recall some essential data of this practice.

1.   In the early Church, from the time of its origin, there existed a general confession of sins, in which people asked God for forgiveness before starting any official form of worship. This practice resembled our *confiteor* or the penitential act with which we start

---

[26] J. RAMOS-REGIDOR: *El sacramento de la penitencia*, Salamanca 1975, p. 203. C. VOGEL: "To enter into penance was equivalent to signing their civil death sentence. Thus, since the end of the fifth century fell into disuse, and the indifference towards it was on the rise" (p. 85).

the eucharistic celebration.[27] The early form however did not constitute sacramental confession.

2. In order to correct vices and practice virtues since the third century, at least there also existed a confession of the sins to a priest or to a spiritual father. As a form of spiritual direction, this practice spread rapidly among the ranks of monks and ascetics. The confession was made to a spiritual teacher, perhaps not even a priest. Although made out of humility and in seeking advice and encouragement for the spiritual life, such confessions do not belong to the realm of the sacrament. Authors like P. Galtier and J. Grotz defended these confessions by concluding that when they were made to the presbyters, they were of sacramental order.[28] Today, however, this conclusion has been dismissed.[29] The early documents refer only to an ecclesiastical or canonical penance for grave sins. Later, in the fifth and sixth centuries some pious Christians requested ecclesiastical penance though they had no grave sins; but this must be considered as an exception.[30]

3. In order to determine the requirements for the valid reception of canonical penance, it has always been mandatory that there is either confession of sins or some manifestation of the motives for requesting public penance. This previous confession to the "entrance into penance" can, by no means,

---

[27] Cf. *Didaché* 4, 14; 14, 1 (*Fathers of the Church*, pp. 82, 91).

[28] Cf. P. GALTIER: *L'Église et la rémission de péchés aux premiers siècles*, Paris 1932; Id. *L'Église et la rémission de péchés aux premiers siècles. A propose de la pénitence primitive*, in RHE 30 (1934) 797-846; Id., *Aux origines du Sacrament de penitence*, Roma 1951; J. GROTZ: *Die Entwicklung des Bußstufenwesen in der vornicänischen Kirche*, Freiburg 1955.

[29] It is common opinion today that in former times it never existed a sacramental penance distinct from the public one. See C. Vogel, K. Rahner, P. Anciaux, Z. Alszeghy, J. Bada, P. Adnès, M. Schmaus, Carra de Vaux Saint-Cyr, H. Rondet, Ramos Regidor, etc.

[30] Cf. VOGEL, op. cit., p. 57; "Some virtuous Christians practiced penance even though they had not committed grave sins. This practice, no matter how paradoxical it may seem at first, has an explanation, as we will see later."

be equated with the detailed confession of sins as imposed by the Council of Trent (Sess. XIV, can. 7; DS 1707). It would be a serious historical error to conclude this, since the circumstances and forms of celebration were quite diverse.

Due to the harshness of the satisfaction demanded from and the obligations imposed on the poor penitent, the tendency was to limit as far as possible the list of sins requiring canonical penance. In general, although it is necessary to take into consideration different periods and places, the sacrament of penance used to be reserved for sins of a very grave and scandalous nature. Some theologians sought to reserve the sacrament for the three capital sins of apostasy, homicide and adultery,[31] but this interpretation did not prevail. Other authors, on the contrary, affirmed that the Church was not able to reconcile persons who committed such sins (Tertullian, in his montanist epoch, and Novatianus).

Many of the sins that demanded the canonical penance were public sins within small Christian communities, such as those common in the first centuries. In such settings, because the sins were already known, it was almost unnecessary to confess them. Because of the massive conversion of pagans to Christianity during the era of Constantine, circumstances changed remarkably and rapidly.

4. The clergy of the fourth century and subsequently also the monks of the fifth century were forbidden from seeking ecclesiastical penance because of its infamous character. Some may ask whether there would be for them no means to obtain forgiveness for their sins. If the integral confession and the priestly absolution were the only ordinary means,[32] we would be forced to arrive at this conclusion.

---

[31] ST. PACIAN is often quoted, *Paraenesis ad paenitentiam*, chapter 5, but it does not seem that Pacian had reduced the public penance to these three sins.

[32] On the penance of clergy and monks, see the invaluable reference in D. FERNÁNDEZ: *El Sacramento de la Reconciliación*, pp. 137-141.

5. In the early practice of penance the essential problem was not so much the confession of sins but the terrible obligations that canonical penance placed on the penitent's entire life. Because of those obligations, the sacrament was refused. While some scholars refer to the shame of confessing sins,[33] almost all of them insist on the difficulties arising from the satisfaction demanded and consequently the mortified life of a penitent. Precisely due to these inhuman penances, the ecclesiastical penance in the fifth century was reserved almost exclusively for the elderly or the terminally ill.

One conclusion is crystal clear: it is an error to affirm that any individual and detailed confession to a priest is the only means for obtaining forgiveness of sins committed after baptism. In olden times, communities practiced quite diverse ways of celebrating the sacrament of penance and these forms can in no way be identified with the present-day private confession. Due to their extraordinarily rigorous and exceptional character, only few Christians practised these early penitential forms. In the early centuries of the Church, countless saints and ordinary Christians did not ever receive the sacrament of penance. During those times, baptism and the eucharist were the two great sacraments for the remission of sins and reconciliation.

Theology

1. Since my early days as a priest I have been deeply impressed by Christ's behavior towards sinners. He was called "the friend of tax collectors and sinners" (Lk 7:34) and He always forgave them freely whenever he met repentant persons. He did not ask the number or the nature of their sins, he

---

[33] See, for example, St. Pacian: "My call is addressed then especially to you, my people, who refuse the penance for the sins you have committed; to you... who are not ashamed to sin and feel ashamed to confess." (Cf. Vogel, p. 137.)

simply demanded of them faith and love. So often a gesture or a word of supplication was enough for Jesus to forgive and absolve: "Go in peace, your faith has saved you" (Lk 7:50; cf. Mt 9:22); "Her many sins are forgiven, because she has loved much" (Lk 7:47).

The deeds and teachings of Jesus entail far more than the decrees of the Council of Trent or any other council. Jesus forgave the public prostitute (Lk 7:36-50), the adulterous woman (Jn 8:1-11), the repentant thief (Lk 23:43). He taught that the publican returned to his house reconciled with God just by shouting: "O God, be merciful to me, a sinner" (Lk 18:13). He taught that the father joyfully welcomed back his prodigal son by forgiving him and then celebrating his return by holding a banquet (Lk 15:11-32).

Whenever I contemplate the Gospels, I ask myself, whether God is demanding more now than what Jesus demanded, or whether God's mercy is somehow less now, or whether God's justice and holiness demand more now.

These questions must be answered with a resounding negative. Whatever Jesus did, he did well. God continues to forgive generously and freely whenever there is a person with the same sincere dispositions. There is no demanding any accurate accounts nor any imposition of difficult conditions. The necessary and essential function of the Church is to help, not to obstruct the person who repents and seeks forgiveness.

2.   From the bestowed offices that the confessor exercises as judge and doctor, theologians have deduced the necessity of the integral confession. In order to pass sentence, the priest as a judge must know the case while as a doctor he must know the sickness in order to heal.

We have already referred to the function of a judge, and how it is to be understood concerning the declaration of sins. Far more preferable is the image of a doctor, who cures and heals the sickness. From this point is deduced the utility, the appropriateness and even the necessity of declaring the sins in order to apply the proper remedy. This is by way of comparison, and by no means is a dogmatic imposition. In reality, in the case of grave sins, we may ask how many seek advice and then follow the confessor's directions, if they confess only once a year. On the contrary, advice and spiritual direction are ordinarily sought by pious persons, who do not usually have grave sins.

The doctor can cure the patients if they reveal to him their pains and symptoms, but if the obligation to declare all grave sins prevents Christians from receiving the sacraments, this injunction is not profitable for their cure. In essence, theologians appeal to a non-existing function in order to impose a grave obligation. For penitents, the consequences deduced from these functions could also be deduced more strictly for the minister. If he is to be of real service to those who resort to him, as a judge and as a doctor the priest needs knowledge not only of theology, but also of psychology and of the spiritual life. If this was required as an indispensable condition, the number of confessors would, of necessity, decrease.

ORIGINS OF THE DETAILED CONFESSION OF ALL THE SINS

At present, the individual and integral confession of all grave sins is taught as an indispensable obligation for obtaining forgiveness of these sins. This gives the wrong impression, as if the obligation were very long standing, even though it is not so. Although referred to the earlier pages, we will now summarize the origin of this precept.

a. *Remote origins.* There once existed a free and spontaneous confession to a priest or to a spiritual father. Clement of Alexandria and Origen already referred to this practice.[34] It

---

[34] Cf. D. FERNÁNDEZ: *El Sacramento de la Reconciliación*, pp. 143-147. The texts of the ancient authors are found in H. KARP: *La pénitence. Textes et Commentaires des origines de l'ordre pénitentiel de l'Eglise ancienne*, Neuchatel 1970.

seems certain however that this private confession was aimed specifically at spiritual direction, or in seeking the most effective means for progress in virtue. Individual and private confession also aimed at determining how necessary it was to submit oneself to ecclesiastical or canonical penance. As I understand the practice, it was not approached as a sacrament. Among the monks of this early period, private confession became an habitual practice of humility or for asking advice from the same elder or the spiritual master, to whom they confided their sins and weaknesses while waiting for a word of encouragement and advice for spiritual advancement. Though St. Basil, St. Benedict and Cassian all refer to this practice as a means for spiritual benefit, it is still not a sacramental confession.

b. Less distant origins. Introduced into the European continent at the beginning of the seventh century, this form of penance was the major source of the custom and obligation to confess all one's sins to a minister. Promoted by the Irish monks who evangelized Europe, the unrepeatability of the sacrament of penance was suppressed and a sanction was established for each sin. For each sin there was a corresponding concrete reparation, and if sins were doubled or tripled, the sanctions were likewise multiplied. This imposed the necessity of accusing oneself of each particular sin and their number.

Although strict regarding the imposed reparations, this system was more bearable than the ancient penance and it quickly spread throughout Europe. Because the sanctions for the committed sins were so strict, multiplying themselves according to the number of sins, the practice became unworkable for a whole lifetime was sometimes not enough to fulfil the required penances.

Soon after the *compensations* and *redemptions* system was introduced which, while mitigating the penance a little, in no way lightened the obligation to accuse oneself of all sins.

Little by little the strictness of reparation for sin was abandoned, while the detailed accusation of one's sins was increasingly considered as substitute for the ancient penances. The actual shame felt at the declaration of sins could be considered a sufficient penance. Thus began the practice of confessing several times the same sins to one priest or to different confessors because through this means the increased shame diminished other forms of penance. Some consequences of this custom have extended right to our present time. Still practiced by many, the re-confession of sins from our past life is founded on two motives: 1) to ensure the matter of the sacrament when persons accuse themselves of faults or imperfections which cannot be considered real sins; 2) to renew and stimulate sincere repentance by considering the sins of one's past life.

When a liturgical custom is introduced, it generally continues for centuries, by which time there is a concerted effort to justify it from Scripture and from theology. This was the same schema in the development of confession of sins. Since the thirteenth century private confession remained practically the only ordinary form of penance; by which time the whole process of the sacrament of penance was called "confession". When in 1215 the Fourth Lateran Council imposed the obligation of confessing and receiving communion at least once a year, the sacrament consisted first of self-examination, then in repentance in telling the sins to a confessor and finally in receiving absolution. Reduced to the minimum, the satisfaction was received before fulfilling the requirements. For this reason the documents of that time inculcate the obligation to confess all grave sins. As a reaction against the Protestants, this trend was further exaggerated by the Council of Trent. It is a serious sacrilege for anyone to consciously omit confessing any grave sin because of shame or fear. Thus we, the older ones and many of our students, have been taught to believe this. Only a study of the history of theology and the wide horizons opened to us by the Second Vatican Council can help to liberate us from clinging to an outdated theology.

The present continual insistence on the integral individual confession as the *only mode* of obtaining the forgiveness of sins is essentially an anachronism. During the first six centuries when it was granted only once in a lifetime or for exceptional cases, the sacrament of penance was no ordinary mode of obtaining forgiveness of sins. It is to be noted too that the anointing of the sick was received less often than now.

In effect, these norms exaggerated the doctrine promulgated by the Council of Trent. The present reason for insisting so much on this issue was the 1972 publication by the Congregation for the Doctrine of the Faith namely the *Pastoral Norms* (AAS 64 [1972] 510-514). They have impeded a deeper and more thorough renewal of the sacrament of penance and continue their negative influence on its celebration. We have pointed out that, in our view, the Pastoral Norms contain a basic historical and theological error. In spite of this they have been adopted by the New Rite of Penance, by the Code of Canon Law and by the apostolic exhortation "Reconciliation and Penance".[35] We hope that these reflections will give rise to a serious discussion and thus contribute to clarifying the evangelical doctrine. Through such a discussion we will eliminate the obstacles to the renewal of the penitential celebration in today's Church.

PASTORAL APPROPRIATENESS

For many years we have been defending the major pastoral advantages of this communal form of celebration if proposed by the hierarchy as the ordinary mode of celebrating the sacrament.[36] Liturgically, this form is the most complete, the most suitable and

---

[35] Cf. *Rite of Penance*, numbers 31-34; *Code of Canon Law*, cc. 960-963; *Reconciliation and Penance*, number 31.

[36] Cf. D. FERNÁNDEZ: *Renovación del sacramento de la penitencia*, Pastoral Misionera (1967), number 4, pp. 45-59; number 5, pp. 54-71; Id.: *Nuevas Perspectivas sobre el Sacramento de la Penitencia*, Valencia 1971, pp. 147-155; Id.: *El Sacramento de la reconciliación*, Valencia 1977, pp. 293-299.

the most coherent one, since the community celebration is not interrupted by any individual confession and absolution. The entire community participates in the celebration through prayer, through listening to the Word, by asking for forgiveness, and then by the public confession of sins and finally by celebrating reconciliation and thanksgiving. This form of celebration does not require many confessors, which is one of the difficulties of the first form (reconciliation of many penitents with individual confession and absolution). If well prepared, Form C (reconciliation of many penitents with general confession and absolution) can be the ideal form for religious communities, seminaries, schools, days of recollection, cursillos, retreats or other gatherings under the direction of one priest. If preceded by careful preparation and a catechesis especially in Advent and in Lent, it will also be the most convenient and most suitable mode for a Christian commitment in parishes. When authorized by the rules, one of these celebrations could become the norm. This extended form even offers the possibility of chronologically spacing out the penitential process through its separate segments. One day can be devoted to the welcome, the listening to the Word of God and examination. Another day can be dedicated to the deepening of repentance, asking for forgiveness and some proposed satisfaction to be fulfilled before receiving absolution. In a third segment the community or the group can again gather joyfully to celebrate their common reconciliation.

That we defend the possibility and convenience of this particular form of celebration does not mean that we do not appreciate other ways of receiving the sacrament, and in particular the individual confession. This last mentioned form satisfies a human need that in turn responds to a deep longing to acknowledge and to confess one's sins in confidence to a person endowed with the power to grant forgiveness in God's name. It is a necessary obligation to provide for all the faithful the possibility of individual sacramental reconciliation. We referred to this earlier[37] and we reaffirm our view that this form

---

[37] *El Sacramento de la reconciliación*, pp. 303-315.

of private celebration must continue to exist, not as an alternative, but as a complementary form. We should not impoverish the sacrament of penance by contending for the validity of only one form of celebration. Each form has its own intrinsic value which it is necessary to optimize for the Christian life of the communities.

CHAPTER 2

Is There an Obligation to Individually Confess Grave Sins after Receiving a General Absolution?

There is a question often posed by both priests and faithful and which must be handled separately: Why confess again sins already forgiven in a community celebration? How can we justify this obligation imposed by the Church?

From its inception this norm has been the object of serious discussion. The *Pastoral Instruction* of the Spanish bishops devotes great attention to it and tries to justify this disciplinary norm not only from the perspective of the norm, but also from the essence of the sacrament (cf. nos. 63 and 64). Clearly this effort is laudable as is the search for the underlying reasons behind the integral personal confession to the priest even after receiving the forgiveness of sins in a community celebration. Some of the reasons presented by this document are not convincing. For example, the document speaks of the need for the Church's mediation or of the need for manifesting outwardly one's conversion. Such need suggests that these elements are not present in a more perfect way in a community celebration. Though other reasons are based on firmer theological foundation, we will not address them here.

Firstly, we must recognize that the present norms impose on the faithful the obligation to confess personally afterwards all grave sins not yet confessed. Those persons who receive a general absolution with only a general confession must be ready to confess in due time all grave sins that in the present circumstances they could not confess (*Pen. Rit.*, no. 33).

Unless a just cause would prevent it, those persons whose grave sins have been forgiven with a common absolution must go to the oral confession before receiving the next general absolution. Whatever the circumstances, unless there is a moral impossibility, those persons still are obliged to approach the confessor within the year.

For this norm the reason is that like all other Christians, "they are also obliged by the precept to confess all their sins individually to a priest at least once a year. In particular, it is understood this includes those grave ones, not yet confessed" (*Pen. Rit.*, no. 34).

Canon 963 of the new code makes this obligation more concrete by explaining that this confession must be made "as soon as possible". "Without prejudice to the obligation presented in Canon 989, those who receive the forgiveness of sins with a general absolution must approach individual confession as soon as possible (*quam primum*) before receiving another general absolution, unless there exists a just cause" (c. 963).

While at present these are the norms, it needs to be added that this clause of imposing the obligation to confess has been restated several times since the Middle Ages. If anyone receives sacramental absolution without the confession of sins and is in danger of death, or suffering from a serious disease, due to the large number of panitents or due to any other impeding cause, after the danger, that person is compelled to make an individual confession. Here let us note two important points:

a. These emergency cases (war, danger of death, a dying person, physical or moral impossibility) present a very different liturgical picture from that of a community penitential celebration which under the direction of a priest is well prepared and conducted without haste.

b. In earlier times, when a sick person in danger of death asked for reconciliation, which was common, it was granted without any difficulty. If that person recovered, what was then demanded was not the integral confession of sins, but the ecclesiastical penance established by the canons. That, of course, was the difficult prescription. We do not hold that regarding their subsequent obligations those emergency cases in the past centuries could be equated with the present-day faithful who voluntarily attend a community penitential celebration.

For a clearer understanding, we are limiting ourselves to a case in which the faithful participate in a community celebration (Form C: reconciliation of several penitents with general confession and community absolution). Why is there imposed on these faithful the obligation of an individual confession afterwards: "in due time," or "as soon as possible" (c. 963) and in any case "before receiving the next general absolution"?

1. It cannot be doubted that the faithful who with proper disposition participate in such celebrations will receive forgiveness of their sins.

2. Therefore, the confession afterwards is not to receive the forgiveness of sins, but is instead a sign or expression of a person's sincere conversion. This later confession could be advised to whoever wished it, but it should not in any way be imposed.

3. There is to be a clear distinction between ecclesiastical discipline and theology. While both should go hand in hand, they do not always do so. The present norms take for granted that the obligation to declare all grave sins to the priest in order

to obtain forgiveness is a divine precept that was solemnly declared at the Council of Trent. We have already been pointed out that this reasoning is incorrect.

4. It is also held that confession is an integral and essential part of the sacrament of penance; and therefore it is inconceivable to omit it. The penitents' confession to a priest however is identified with the individual and complete accusation of all their grave sins. This second part is neither accurate nor true. The act of recognizing ourselves as sinners before God and before the Church can take different forms.

5. It is highly desirable that these norms should be changed as soon as possible, but since such dispositions continue to bind, we cannot but respect them and abide by them.

6. Although I hold that they are not accurate, since these dispositions do exist, the theologians and bishops in the *Pastoral Instruction* merely seek an acceptable explanation of them. This they do instead of questioning their very theological foundation. I would argue that in the *Doctrinal Orientations* of the Spanish bishops added to the *Rite of Penance,* they have given quite a satisfactory explanation (nos. 64 and 80): "The confession of sins," they assert, "is an important part of the normal process of reconciliation, and as such it is valued; in the case of a general absolution, the confession of sins can be placed after the absolution, notwithstanding its penitential meaning" (no. 64, p. 37).

"The confession of sins, as a personalizing segment of the penitential celebration, is the element of this sacrament on which the pastoral has focused its particular attention for centuries. It is necessary therefore to help it regain its corresponding place in the whole" (*ibid.*). This means that the accusation of sins and confession do not become the sole elements of the sacrament. They have been accorded too much importance in pastorals and even now they are still being given the same emphasis in ecclesiastical ordinances.

In referring expressly to this confession after a community celebration, they read: "The meaning of this confession is not to obtain the forgiveness of sins, but is a penitential act that expresses conversion, and the petition for help and enlightenment from the minister of the sacrament, for assistance in the concrete situation of life" (no. 8, pp. 45-56). The pastorals rightly note: "The sacramental efficacy of this form of reconciliation is not conditioned by the confession afterwards, although the penitent should be ready to make it, if he has the awareness of having committed grave sins" (no. 76, p. 44).

With some norms given by the Holy See all this seems quite reasonable and correct from our present situation. The most reasonable thing, however, would be for such ordinances to change in any forthcoming legislation. From this perspective of the unquestionable fact of the obligation to confess afterwards as imposed by the Code of Canon Law, there must be the effort of the *Pastoral Instruction* to justify these norms from theology and from pastoral reflection (cf. nos. 63-64).

WHY IT SEEMS THAT CHANGING THE LEGISLATION WOULD BE MOST CORRECT AND MOST REASONABLE

The Fundamental Question

a. Is there any divine precept to declare all sins to the priest in order to receive forgiveness? We have already said that such a precept does not exist.

b. Is the confession of sins an integral and essential part of the sacrament of penance?

While we can answer positively, the confession of sins, as an act of faith and of hope in forgiveness, should not be identified with the obligation to declare to the minister all mortal sins not yet confessed. There are, in fact, many forms of confessing sins before God and before the Church. Tears are a more eloquent and heartfelt language than words. Dressing oneself in sackcloth and wearing a hairshirt or covering one's head with ashes and asking for prayers from the faithful at the

church's door were impressive forms of confession of sins
before the entire ecclesial community. Today, participating in
a penitential act and asking God and the community for
forgiveness of sins is an adequate confession, because as
such, it contains more religious and ecclesial meaning than the
secret confession to the priest.

    c. Does the secret confession to the priest have any pastoral
advantages? No doubt it has, and many. We must here
distinguish:

> 1. To many persons, being able to liberate themselves
>   from the conscience of sin by confessing to a priest and
>   then receiving absolution is a necessity and a relief,
>   because in a personal confession one can find relief,
>   peace and consolation. Suppressing or abandoning this
>   practice would be quite wrong.
>
> 2. To many other persons, the obligation to confess their
>   sins to the priest is a hindrance that keeps them away
>   from the sacrament. To still others it becomes a night-
>   mare or a torment. Because many devout persons have
>   developed neurosis and psychological diseases, it is
>   not honest to close our eyes to these realities.

Based on these reasons, I believe that the confession of one's
sins to a priest as the Church's representative in order to
receive sacramental reconciliation is something good and to
be commended. It helps us to make a serious examination and
a deeper repentance to achieve a more personal and existential commitment to amendment. It also is a source of support
and encouragement for overcoming many difficulties in one's
Christian life.

But imposing this confession of all sins as an obligation and
believing that to do otherwise means no possible forgiveness
leads to forgetting the serious consequences of this law. I
consider this approach to be both unjust and detrimental to
persons. Nor should it be forgotten that for any person seeking

reconciliation there are many diverse ways and means for outwardly expressing repentance and acknowledging oneself as a sinner before the Church and before God.

With this Understanding There is Already a More Relevant Answer to the Question Proposed at the Outset

Because what God has forgiven is forgiven forever, it would be more just and reasonable to suppress the obligation of confession after the community sacramental absolution. If they have the correct disposition, Christians who participate in a community penitential celebration fully receive forgiveness and reconciliation with God and with the Church. Those persons will have fulfilled all the requirements imposed by the sacrament in a more perfect way than in private confession. Why impose on them new obligations? If imposed for their sins, only the satisfaction can have any meaning towards a fuller configuration with Christ. At most it could be concluded that the "general confession" of these celebrations is more *expressive.*

Because there is no divine precept or obligation *de iure divino* to declare all grave sins to a priest, there is a further significant consequence. When it is affirmed that there can be no true contrition without including the intention of confessing all sins afterwards, this presupposes that there exists a divine precept for confessing all grave sins to the confessor. This we deny. Thus though hardly admissable theologically, the excessive strictness of Canon 962 disappears, and with it the ordinance concerning the necessity of an intention to confess afterwards in order to gain sacramental absolution.

As an expression of a true conversion, confession is sufficiently expressed in a whole community celebration for it expressly includes a general confession of sins. If this was judged to be insufficient, the rite of this celebration could be slightly re-designed, without obliging anyone to a confession afterwards.

The priest must always be ready and available to receive the faithful in private and to fulfill his mission in the spirit of Jesus. This mission is exercised by the priest and is understood that he is father and doctor and teacher for all who come to him. This approach does not justify the ordinance of obliging all Christians to accuse oneself of all one's grave sins. Presently such an obligation extends even to those who have already been reconciled with God and with the Church.

CHAPTER 3

Penance and Eucharist

It is acceptable to speak nowadays of the eucharist as a *sacrament for the forgiveness of sins.* We should perhaps say that this view has not sufficiently penetrated the minds of the faithful nor the ordinary catechesis, because within the last years several authors have dealt with this question.[1] On the contrary, the ancient authors and even those in the Middle Ages gave much importance to this aspect of *purification* and

---

[1] D. A. TANGHE: *L'Eucharistie pour la rémission des péchés,* Irenikon 34 (1961), 165-181; J. M. R. TILLARD: *The Bread and the Cup of Reconciliation, Concilium 7*(1971/1) 38-54; Idem: *L'Eucharistie, Pâque de l'Église,* Paris, 1964; Idem: *Pénitence et eucharistie,* LMD 90 (1967), 103-131; J. A. GRACIA: *La Eucaristía como purificación y perdón de los pecados, en los textos litúrgicos primitivos,* Phase 7 (1967), 65-77; J. RAMOS-REGIDOR: *El sacramento de la penitencia,* Salamanca, 1975, pp. 367-375; D. FERNÁNDEZ: *El sacramento de la reconciliación,* Valencia, 1977, pp. 204-210; J. L. LARRABE: *Reconciliación y penitencia en la misión de la Iglesia,* Madrid, 1983, pp. 213-223; J. M. R. TILLARD: *El pan y el cáliz de la reconciliación,* Concilium 7 (1971/I), 35-51; P. BROWE: *Die Kommunionvorbereitung im Mittelalter,* ZKTh 56 (1932) 375-415; N. MARTÍN RAMOS: *La Eucaristía, misterio de reconciliación,* Communio (Comentarios internacionales de Eclesiología y Teología, Sevilla) XXIII (1990) 31-73; 209-248; 333-354.

propitiation within the eucharistic celebrations. The Council of Trent also was aware of the need to proclaim *the propitiatory character of the sacrifice of the Mass* to those who participate in it with a true spirit of contrition and penance[2] for it forgives sins and crimes no matter how grave they may be. This was declared in the 22nd session on the Eucharist, in order to refute the Protestant doctrine which affirmed that the Mass is neither a sacrifice nor an oblation for sins. For the Protestants, the Mass is a memorial of the Lord's supper and the commemoration of the sacrifice of the cross. As such it amounts to the testament and the promise of forgiveness of sins. As a sacrifice, however, the Mass has no benefit for the living or for the dead.[3] As against this position it is understandable that these denials moved the Council of Trent to ratify the forgiving value of the sacrifice of the Mass. But the question cannot limit itself to the meaning of the texts of the Council of Trent. By the sixteenth century most of the value was lost that the ancient Fathers attributed to the eucharist as a sacrament of reconciliation and for the forgiveness of sins. In this earlier period sacramental penance was an exception, for after baptism, the eucharist was the great sacrament of pardon for ordinary sins. Only later did the sacrament of penance take over from the other sacraments this function of forgiveness. During the Middle Ages the *penitential pilgrimage* was but one of the ecclesial forms of penance and of the reception of forgiveness. It was one official way of obtaining forgiveness which lasted approximately from the ninth up to the twelfth century.[4] Although without an official character, the pilgrimage as a penance for sins had started much earlier.

In the fifth or sixth century when the pilgrims arrived in Rome or Jerusalem or some other place of pilgrimage, they partici-

---

[2] Sess. XXIII, chap. 2 ; DS 1743; COLLANTES 1077.

[3] Cf. CT, VII, Act. pars IV, vol. 1, pp. 375-376.

[4] Cf. F. BOURDEAU: *El camino del perdón*, chap. 2, Peregrinos de la Edad Media, Estella, 1983, pp. 49-75.

pated in the eucharist because they were considered sufficiently forgiven. The eucharist was understood as *sealing this
forgiveness and reconciliation*. Did these pilgrims also receive
the sacrament of penance or another rite of reconciliation
before participating in the eucharist? Before the seventh
century they certainly did not receive sacramental or ecclesial
penance. The ancient texts do not show the pilgrims asking
for or receiving sacramental absolution to be able to participate in the divine mysteries. Rather they considered that the
pilgrimage itself was a sufficient penance and a suitable
ordinance for forgiveness. The eucharist was the "pilgrim's
passover" and therefore the sign of reconciliation and liberation from sin.[5]

SACRED SCRIPTURES

Can we discover the eucharist's character of reconciliation in
the Sacred Scriptures themselves? In the synoptics the accounts of the institution of the eucharist (Mt 26:21-25; Mk
14:18-21; Lk 22:21-23) clearly refer to the "blood shed for the
forgiveness of sins," or "shed for many" or "for you". John
himself (Jn 6:51-58) refers several times to the bread which
will be given them, which "is his flesh for the life of the world"
(6:51). One of Paul's most ancient narratives (1 Cor 11:23-26)
mentions the "body which is broken for you". We do not wish
to develop this point, but only to recall that the actual accounts
of the institution of the eucharist present it as *a sacrament for
the forgiveness of sins*.

Some authors wanted to read this concept into the meals
which Jesus took with tax collectors and sinners, for in them
the forgiveness of sins is mentioned: the banquet given to
Jesus and his disciples by Levi (Lk 5:29), the meal in Zaccheus'
house (Lk 19:1-10), the forgiveness of the woman during the

---

[5] Ibid., pp. 30-31.

meal in Simon the Pharisee's house (Lk 7:36-50), the parable of the prodigal son (Lk 15:11-32), etc. In their presentation, these accounts seem to allude to the eucharistic celebration of the first communities, and in this way they could be a sign, not a proof, that the fraternal meals of the first Christians also recalled the forgiveness of sins.

THE ANCIENT CHURCH

What do the texts of the Fathers and the ancient oriental or western liturgies tell us about the eucharist as a sacrament of forgiveness?

Regarding the *liturgy* we will limit ourselves to selecting some data from D. A. Tanghe's study in *Irenikon:*

> The theologians will have to explain how the eucharist produces these effects, but there is no doubt that in the Leonian, Gelasian and Gregorian sacramentaries it is said that the eucharist is the remission of sins (*absolutio, venia, liberatio*). It cleanses and purifies the soul (*purgatio, mundatio, purificatio*). It is satisfaction for the offense made to God (*expiatio, satisfactio*) and it leaves our soul healed and holy (*sanctificatio, sanitas, salus*).[6]

In the ninth century a Council of Rouen prescribes the following formula for distributing the communion hosts: "May the body and blood of the Lord be profitable to you *for the forgiveness of sins* and for eternal life."[7]

---

[6] Cf. D. A. TANGHE, quot. art., p. 167. On the Leonian, Gelasian and Gregorian sacramentaries cf. E. JANOT: *L'Eucharistie dans les sacramentaires occidentaux,* RSR 17 (1927), 5-24. On this purifying effect attributed to the eucharist, mainly in its own prayers, see the article by J. A. GRACIA: *La eucaristía como purificación y perdón de los pecados en los textos litúrgicos primitivos,* Phase 7 (1967), 65-77.

[7] TANGHE, art. cit., p. 167.

The *Verona Sacramentary*, which was composed between the fourth and sixth centuries, often refers to the eucharist as a medicine and a remedy against sin in affirming that it expiates and purifies our faults. And this is said not of a previous celebration, but of each eucharistic celebration itself:

"Forgive me, O Lord, our iniquities, we beseech you and make us love justice so that we may deserve to receive your gifts."[8]

Even in many prayers after communion in the present-day Roman Missal we ask that the eucharist may deliver us from our sins and make us participants in everlasting life. In the Syrian-Oriental liturgy, for centuries up to the present time, the following formula has been used to distribute the hosts:

"The body of our Lord Jesus Christ for the pious faithful N.N. *for the forgiveness of your sins;* the blood of Christ *for the forgiveness of your sins and for everlasting life.*"[9]

There is no doubt that these formulae express both a conviction and a theology.

The texts of the early Fathers of the Church speak of the purifying and forgiving power of the eucharist and are much more abundant. Here we offer a selection from some authors.

One of the authors who insists more on this character is Ambrose of Milan (333-397). He has a large number of unmistakable testimonies on the Eucharist's purifying and forgiving power.

While not ignoring that humankind continually falls into sin, he comments:

---

[8] Cf. P. SORCI: *L'Eucaristia per la remissione dei peccati. Ricerca nel sacramentario Veronense.* Istituto Superiore di Scienze Religiose, Palermo, 1979, p. 328.

[9] Cf. BRIGHTMAN: *Liturgies Eastern and Western,* Oxford, 1896, p. 298. Quoted by D. A. TANGHE, p. 168.

"If every time that his blood is shed, it is shed for the forgiveness of sins, I have to receive him always, so that he always forgives my sins. If I continually sin, I must always have a remedy."[10]

Ambrose could not offer the sacrament of penance as a remedy for frequent sins because in his time it was received only once in a lifetime and it was reserved for the most serious sins. Hence he resorts to the eucharist as the great means to free us from our sins:

"Every time you drink, you receive the forgiveness of sins and you are permeated with the Spirit."[11]

And a little earlier he wrote:

"Those who ate the manna, died, those who eat from this body will obtain forgiveness of sins and will not die anymore."[12]

One author who has studied in detail *Saint Ambrose of Milan* concludes: "For Ambrose the eucharist has in itself a redeeming power capable of forgiving sins. It is offered in remission of sins and every time we receive the body and blood of Christ, we receive the forgiveness of sins."[13]

In the Orient *Theodore of Mopsuestia* (+428) teaches the common doctrine that the eucharist forgives everyday sins and weaknesses, but then he also refers to the grave sins which

[10] *De Sacramentis*, IV, 6, 28; SChr 25, p. 87.

[11] Ibid., V, 3, 17; SChr 25, p. 92.

[12] Ibid., IV, 4, 24; SChr 25, p. 86.

[13] R. JOHANNY: *L'Eucharistie, centre de l'histoire du salut chez saint Ambroise de Milan*, Paris, 1968, 188; cf. B. STUDER: *L'Eucaristia, remissione dei peccati secondo Ambrogio di Milano*, in the work *Catechesis battesimale e riconciliazione nei Padri del IV secolo* (a cura di S. Felici), Las-Roma, 1984, pp. 65-79.

should be submitted to the canonical penance. He also affirms them saying:

> "I will say without hesitation that if any person has committed those great sins, but decides to abandon evil and to surrender herself/himself to virtue following Christ's precepts, she/he will participate in Christ's mysteries, convinced that she/he will receive the forgiveness of all her/his sins."[14]

Finally let us quote from *Cyril of Alexandria* (+444):

> "I have examined myself and I have found myself unworthy. To those who say thus I say: And when will you be worthy? When will you then presènt yourselves before Christ? And if your sins hinder you from approaching him and if you will never stop falling, who knows their own guilt? The psalm says: will you be left without participating in the sanctification that gives life for eternity? Take then the decision to live a better and more honest life and then participate in the *eulogia* believing that it has the power not only to preserve you from death, but even from diseases."[15]

Although earlier, this testimony by Abbot Pimen, gathered in a Syriac manuscript of the National Library of Paris, also has relevance:

> "Abbot Pimen used to say: The sins committed *before baptism* are forgiven by the purifying nature of baptism, according to what was said: 'Each of you must repent and

---

[14] Cf. TONNEAU-DEVREESSE: *Les Homélies catéchétiques de Théodore de Mopsueste*, Studi e Testi 145 (Città del Vaticano, 1949). Hom-XVI, 34, p. 589.

[15] In S. Joh. IV, 2; PG 73, 584-585.

be baptized in the name of Jesus Christ, so that your sins
may be forgiven' (Acts 2:38).

The sins committed *after Baptism* (are forgiven) by the
holy mysteries of the body and blood of our Lord: 'This is
my body and this is my blood, which is broken and shed
for the forgiveness of sins.' They will be forgiven in the
following way: if they are sins which the Holy Scriptures
severely condemn and are so grave that Paul orders to
exclude from the Kingdom of heaven all those who commit them, those sins are forgiven when, *after a certain time
of (penance) in sackcloth and ashes* according to the laws
and the canons imposed on the transgressors by the
superiors, *the communion is received with a heart* full of
sorrow for their transgressions. But in the case of faults
committed against the brethren, if with all humility they
make a *metania*,[16] asking for forgiveness with repentance,
God immediately forgives, because he said: 'Reconcile
yourself with your brother and sister' and 'Forgive and you
will be forgiven'."[17]

The author distinguishes here three modes of forgiveness of
sins: a) the sins committed before baptism; b) the grave sins
committed after baptism; and c) the light faults that we commit
everyday. Only the second category can offer some difficulty.
For those sins which according to Paul exclude us from the
Kingdom of heaven penance must be done according to the
canons. Here, the author refers, no doubt, to the ancient
ecclesiastical penance. But the interesting side of this text is
that true forgiveness and true reconciliation are not attributed

[16] Latin transcription, slightly modified from the Greek word "metánoia"
which means penance or repentance. It was introduced into Medieval
Latin and meant an act of humiliation, genuflection, prostration. Cf. A.
BLAISE, Dictionaire Latin-Français des auteurs du Moyen Age.

[17] KMOSKO: *Liber graduum*, Patr. Syr. III, p. II-III. It seems an interpo-
lation by a Medieval copyist. A more complete quotation can be seen in
P. SORCI, op. cit., p. 278, n. 63.

to the works of penance, nor to the priestly absolution. "They are forgiven when receiving communion" with hearts full of sorrow for their transgressions.

It is not the rite of penance that the author emphasizes, but the reception of the eucharist to which he attributes the power to forgive and to purify from sins.

Let us finish this series of testimonies with two medieval authors. *Gregory of Bergamo* (+1146) clearly states: "Through this sacrament, piously received, we undoubtedly obtain the forgiveness of sins and we come close to Christ by eating and drinking his blood."[18]

St. Thomas, on the contrary, does not conceal that those who receive the eucharist in mortal sin do not receive the forgiveness of their sins because they have an impediment to receive the effect of this sacrament. This does not mean though that he denies that the eucharist by itself has the power to forgive all sins: "I answer by saying that the power of this sacrament can be considered under two modes. First in itself, in this mode this sacrament has the power to forgive all sins through Christ who is the fountain and the cause of the forgiveness of sins."[19] The other consideration refers to the recipient who can impede the efficacy of the sacrament to attain its effect in the recipient. One thing is clear: since ancient times there has existed a theology that attributes to the reception of Christ's body and blood the effect of forgiving all types of sins. In the ancient authors, the unworthy who receive the sacrament are not the common sinners, but rather those who do not have faith, those who do not recognize the Lord's body, because they then eat and drink their own condemnation (cf. 1 Cor 11:29). Today we could repeat the sentences of the *Expositio Officiorum Ecclesiae*, an ancient book of the Syrian church: "Some have not understood that communion is given to sinners for the forgiveness of sins."[20]

---

[18] *Tractatus de veritate corporis Christi*, ch. 20.
[19] S. Theol. III, q. 79, a. 3.
[20] CSCO, *Script. syri, series II, tom. 92*, trad. vol. I, pp. 69-70.

COUNCIL OF TRENT

We do not deny the importance of the Council of Trent's doctrine, but it must not be considered as the last word. The council met for about 18 years, dealing with the eucharist and with the penance in different sessions. Between the 13th-14th (1551) and 22nd (1562) sessions there is a gap of some ten years. The pope as well as several bishops and theologians had been replaced by new ones. The problems to be solved in these later sessions were also different, hence no one should be surprised that among the texts of the same council there are quite distinct and different aspects and emphases.

In the 13th session, chapter 7 (DS 1647) the council pronounces itself without hesitation on the necessity to "confess" before receiving communion, if the faithful have the consciousness of any mortal sin:

> "The Church's custom proves that this examination is necessary so that without a previous sacramental confession any persons who have the consciousness of a mortal sin do not approach the sacred eucharist, no matter how contrite they may consider themselves. The holy council has decreed that this must always be observed by all Christians, even by priests who are obliged by their office to celebrate, supposing that they do not lack a confessor. But in the case due to an urgent necessity when a priest celebrated without a previous confession, he must confess as soon as possible."

This norm which is so clear and so often repeated throughout the following centuries does not solve all the cases. We must consider other conciliar texts in order to see the whole of the doctrine. Ten years later, in focusing on the sacrifice of the Mass in the 22nd session, chapter 2 (DS 1743) the council affirms:

"The holy council teaches that this sacrifice is truly propitiatory and that through it we can obtain mercy and grace to be helped in due time (Heb 4:16), if we approach God with a sincere heart, with real faith, with fear and reverence, contrite and penitent. Because the Lord is placated by this oblation, in granting the grace and the gift of penance, he forgives the crimes and the sins, no matter how serious they may be. Because the victim is only one and the same, the one who now offers himself through the priestly ministry is the one who earlier offered himself on the cross; only the mode of offering is different."

This doctrine has also been recalled in recent documents of the magisterium and has been widely used in the *Doctrinal and Pastoral Orientations* of the Spanish bishops in the Rite of Penance (no. 67). The bishops note that the intimate relationship between the eucharist and penance does not mean that the sacramental confession must precede the eucharist, unless there is the consciousness of a mortal sin. In order to participate in the eucharist, it is required of Christians that their spirit be a communion of faith and love in the Lord who offers himself to the Father (*Pen. Rit.*, no. 67). Even in the case of grave sin, if the faithful are sincerely repentant and do not find some confessors and there is a spiritual urgency to participate in the eucharist, they may fruitfully approach to receive holy communion (*ibid.*).

In this commentary two different issues are mixed:

1) The eucharistic celebration, participated in with the proper disposition, forgives sins no matter how grave. This is a *doctrinal affirmation* that we have seen confirmed by the liturgical testimonies and by the texts of the Fathers.

2) Since the Council of Trent, and even before, the Church prescribes that the faithful who have the consciousness of a mortal sin must receive the sacramental absolution, if possible, before approaching communion.[21] This is a disciplinary norm.

---

[21] We do not mean to present here the abundant legislation prior to Trent on the obligation to confess before communion. Cf. L. BRAECKMANS:

For a better understanding we are omitting the exceptions, cases of grave urgency to celebrate or to receive communion, in order to limit ourselves to the general norm.

HOW IS THE QUESTION PRESENTED TODAY?

Today, unfortunately, the question is presented in a more practical and pastoral context, but also in a much more banal context. Instead of exploring deeply the meaning of reconciliation and the most profound meaning of confession, as an expression of an authentic conversion, the problem that perplexes today's priests and faithful is this: *Having the consciousness of a grave sin, may holy communion be received with an act of contrition, before going to confession?* They all seek a clear answer, without any ambiguities.

This question really contains a simple reply.

From the Norms, the Answer is Clear

a. As a *general rule* it is necessary to receive sacramental absolution before communion, if there is any consciousness of a grave sin. It is not sufficient to make an act of perfect contrition. Reconciliation with God and with the Church demands this clear act of sacramental penance.

b. As an *exception*, if there is a real necessity to receive communion or to celebrate, and there is no facility to find a confessor, the priest or the faithful may celebrate or receive communion by making an act of perfect contrition and by being prepared to make a sacramental confession afterwards, at the earliest opportunity. Cases of grave and urgent necessity are not specifically determined by the law.

Confession et communion au moyen âge et au Concile du Trente. Duculot, 1971; J. L. LARRABE: *Reconciliación y penitencia en la misión de la Iglesia,* Madrid, 1983, pp. 217-233.

This Answer, so Clear from the Disciplinary Norms Is Not Theologically Satisfactory

Let us proceed section by section. The Church norms are quite clear and concrete. Since before the Fourth Lateran Council (1215) and before the Council of Trent (1545-1563) there already existed this norm that the faithful who had some consciousness of a mortal sin should receive the sacrament of Penance before receiving communion. Let us recall some ordinances since the Council of Trent.

    a.   Session XIII, chapter 7 (DS 1647); Canon 11 (DS 1661).

    b.   Code of Canon Law (by Benedict XV, year 1918) c. 856: "Let anyone who has the consciousness of a mortal sin not approach holy communion, without a previous sacramental confession, no matter how much sorrow or contrition they possess; in the case of an urgent necessity, if there is no confessor, make first an act of a perfect contrition."

This refers to the faithful. For the priests there is quite a similar canon (c. 807), but they are warned to confess afterwards "as soon as possible". These sentences are copied almost literally from the Trent text.

    c.   New Code of Canon Law (by John Paul II, year 1983) c. 916: "Anyone who is conscious of grave sin may not celebrate Mass or receive the Body of the Lord without previously having been to sacramental confession, unless there is a grave reason and there is no opportunity to confess; in this case the person is to remember the obligation to make an act of perfect contrition, which includes the resolve to go to confession as soon as possible."

This canon is meant for priests and the faithful, and makes clear for both, not only for the priests, that they must confess *as soon as possible.* Aside from the explanations of the theologians, these norms are being repeated in many documents of the *magisterium* up to the present day. Therefore we consider it necessary to quote them in particular. Let us just recall that the apostolic exhortation *Reconciliation and Penance* says in no. 27: "It is necessary nevertheless, to recall that the Church, guided by the faith in this great sacrament, teaches that no Christian can receive the eucharist before obtaining God's forgiveness if the person is conscious of a great sin.... Those who want to receive communion should remember the precept: *Let each one, then, examine himself/herself* (1 Cor 11:28). And the Church's tradition shows that this test is necessary so that nobody, conscious of being in mortal sin – although considering himself/herself to have repented, can approach the sacred eucharist without a previous sacramental confession."

Eucharisticum Mysterium by Paul VI, AAS 59 (1967) 560 is quoted, but in fact the text is a copy of the Council of Trent's ordinances. There can be no doubt concerning the Church's general norm.

There continue to be the *exceptional cases* of grave or urgent necessity, which are not enumerated in detail in those norms. The simplest case is that of priests who cannot fail to celebrate the eucharist without giving scandal to the faithful. As it concerns ordinary Christians it refers to a grave or urgent necessity to receive communion in order not to be involuntarily deprived for a long time of the holy communion. This may happen in mission fields as well as in our First World. There may be a case where members of the faithful who, not having the opportunity to confess for a lack of a priest, have to spend long periods without receiving the eucharist, if they did not avail themselves of a priest's visit. Nowadays, if we refer only to the communion and not to the sacrament of penance, the case would be rare, because laypeople also have authority to distribute communion. Nevertheless, there are cases when communion seems quite convenient or necessary and cannot be received, because persons had no prior opportunity to confess. For example, it may be the first reception of communion by a son or daughter, at a wedding, an important family feast, a priestly ordination, a religious who lives in community and has not had the opportunity to receive the sacrament of reconciliation. In all these cases and in others similar to these the Church allows persons to approach holy communion, without a previous sacramental confession, but those persons must have the intention and do have the obligation to confess afterwards in due time. Unfortunately, the new Code in the above mentioned Canon 916 says that it must be done "as soon as possible", when it would have sufficed just saying "in due time" as is said in Canon 962 for those who have received an individual general absolution of their sins.

The bishops' *Pastoral Instruction* in an understanding and generous spirit adds in note 177 of no. 70: "On the obligation to go to confession as soon as possible, the classical moral norms took into consideration particularly the case of the priests who must celebrate Mass, but now it would also seem to apply as well to laypeople, given the emphasis today to *full participation* in the reception of the eucharistic communion." There is no difficulty, then, concerning the present norms. But there is still another question as to whether these norms fully accord with theology. I do not think so. Let us add, nevertheless, that the early Church Fathers, although strict in proposing the obligation to confess before communion, were generously understanding in the application of these exceptional cases. For example, they admit as not finding an adequate confessor, who inspires confidence, a sufficient cause,[22] or feeling a deep devotion to receive communion on a feastday without having had the opportunity to confess previously. Thomas Aquinas goes so far as allowing that some inspiration from God, inviting a person to receive communion, would be a sufficient reason for someone to approach communion before the sacramental reconciliation; provided that the person is contrite and has had no opportunity to confess.[23] As we can see, the applications are wide enough.

---

[22] Cf. RICHARD DE MEDIAVILLA, In IV Sent. (Lyon 1527) f. 114.
[23] Cf. BRAECKMANS, op. cit., p. 49.

What Does Theology Say?

As has often happened in the history of the sacrament of
penance, the canonical norms have not been able to solve the
real problems. Something similar is happening to this question: the norms are clear but they take for granted that there are
only two categories of sins: *mortal* and *venial*, which distinction is incomplete and imperfect. There is such a wide discrep-
ancy in contents and gravity among different mortal sins that
it is not possible to include them all under a common de-
nominator. Nor is it possible to categorize them regarding their
consequences and, particularly, regarding the question as to
whether or not any one after having committed a mortal sin
may receive communion after making an act of sincere
repentance. I believe that at least we should distinguish three
categories of sin in order to offer a realistic and reasonable
solution.

It is not for me to pinpoint the changes or the characteristics
of the new Christian morality, which is a morality not of law and
sin but a morality of love, of the evangelical values in imitation
of Christ. All these developments presuppose and also demand a new perception of sin in its ethical and religious or
transcendent dimension. As a foundation for the triple direction of sin, I would here like to allude to the three clearly
distinguished levels in human action:

- *The fundamental option* is a deep and constant orien-
  tation, freely adopted by a person, which gives meaning to all one's work. It affects a person's deepest
  nucleus, committing that person to a determined, and
  to a certain extent definitive, direction in life.[24]

- *The attitude* proceeds from the fundamental option
  and looks at a determined value: fidelity, love, justice,
  friendship, compassion.

---

[24] Cf. FIDEL HERRÁEZ: *La opción fundamental,* Salamanca, 1978.

- *The act* is the result or expression of the attitude in a determined moment. It can ratify the attitude, or run counter to it, in sin, if the fundamental attitude was good.

According to these principles we distinguish three kinds of sins:

a. *Mortal sins.* They destroy our fundamental option for God and the community. They are acts that presuppose a state of sin in which the person makes do without moral or ethical laws. "The mortal sin is a refusal of God or of love; it is doing without what faith, hope and charity demand from us; it is putting as the maximum principle in our life not God or love, but our egoism, or ourselves, above everything else."[25]

b. *Grave sins.* They are also called "sins of weakness".[26] Grave sins are those that deeply transform a good attitude, while at the same time threatening to change or to destroy the fundamental option without destroying it. These sins seriously damage our fundamental option, and therefore demand from us a refusal and a sincere conversion.

Frequently, they are not more than an inconsistency with respect to our fundamental option for God and the community, or some weakness in a moment of passion or of weakness, but they do not presuppose a refusal of God nor of love as a fundamental attitude in our life.

c. *Light sins.* They are those acts that do not change the fundamental option of our life nor seriously threaten it. They

---

[25] Cf. D. BOROBIO: *Es necesario confesarse... ¿todavía?*, Bilbao, 1971, p. 39; Idem: *El sacramento de la reconciliación*, Bilbao, 1975, pp. 23-25; L. BERTSCH: *Buße und Bußsakrament in der heutigen Kirche*, Mainz, 1970, pp. 26-28.

[26] In the quoted book in the preceding note *El sacramento de la reconciliación*, page 24, D. Borobio points out that in this booklet he prefers to refer to "sins of weakness or of fragility" not to confuse the "grave sins" with the "mortal sins", which the official documents identify.

diminish charity in us, but do not break our relationship with God or with the Church.

Bearing these principles in mind, the question whether one can receive communion without a previous confession is much easier to consider:

1. It is evident that any one who has *mortal sin* may not participate in the eucharist, unless one first undergoes conversion and receives the sacrament of reconciliation. Such sins are incompatible with communion.

2. Those who have *grave sins* as a fruit of weakness or of a moment of confusion but are sincerely repentant may approach communion before receiving sacramental absolution. They are sorry for having failed and ask forgiveness from God or from the offended community/ member. Their attitude is of love and not of hatred, of communion and not of severing it. They therefore possess the necessary dispositions to participate in the eucharist.

3. *Light sins.* These sins do not arouse problems regarding communion, because we know that they are forgiven in many ways and there is no obligation to confess them.

This *triple distinction* is easy and instead of creating problems for people it solves them, especially for pious and scrupulous persons who often ask these questions. To affirm that rarely does a Christian commit a "mortal sin" is not the best solution, nor is reducing most sins to "venial sins", if only two kinds of sins are distinguished. There are "grave" sins regarding the matter, which are a fruit of weakness, or of occasion, or of human weakness. The persons who commit them immediately repent of their actions and do not wish to break away from God or from the Church. They are firmly resolved that as long as they are capable they will avoid sin in the future. These persons possess the due dispositions for a full participation in the eucharist. But it is obvious that as long as sinners do not show signs of conversion and receive the sacrament of reconciliation, this norm cannot be applied to any scandalous, public, or very grave sins, for example, concubinage, adultery, homicide, refusal of faith, rape, public scandal.

Many persons suffer from scruples in receiving communion, thinking that they have not promptly refused some bad thought. While it could be said that there has been no grave sin, it could also be said: "Although your sin has been grave, it has been an act of weakness that has not changed your attitude towards God nor towards the community. If you really repent and wish to avoid all sins and the occasions of sin in the future, you can in conscience receive communion. It is enough if you accuse yourself in your next confession, if you consider the matter to be grave." Nowadays the problem is not so large as it was years ago and perhaps there is too much laxity in approaching communion without previously receiving the sacrament of penance. Essentially the remedy is not making the norms more stringent, but in forming and educating the faithful. The distinction between m*ortal sins* and *grave sins* or *sins of weakness* can help solve difficulties, supposing always that the penitent is really repentant.

Various Sacramental Forms to Celebrate Conversion

The present rite of the sacrament of penance presents three sacramental modes for obtaining forgiveness and for celebrating the sacrament of penance. This is not to forget the existence of other extra-sacramental means which also grant forgiveness of sins. There are other sacraments of reconciliation besides — baptism, the eucharist, and the anointing of the sick. Here, however, we are dealing with only the sacrament of penance. The official forms are three:

Form A: Rite to reconcile a penitent alone.

Form B: Rite to reconcile various penitents with individual confession and absolution.

Form C: Rite to reconcile many penitents with general confession and absolution.

For reason of brevity we sometimes refer to *Form A, B* or *C* in abbreviation without explaining the contents.

FORM A: RECONCILIATION OF A PENITENT ALONE

Unexplored Possibilities of This Rite

This traditional form has been in use throughout the last centuries, and appears with remarkable modifications in the new Rite, although with far fewer in daily practice. This form offers many possibilities which have not yet been appropriately used. To be realistic, however, as presented in the new Rite, it can be performed in all its details only a few times. It is possible only when the penitent looks for the adequate time and place for a peaceful confession in some room. The confessional is not a suitable place for this rite. The new Code of Canon Law, however, prescribes anew the confessional as the ordinary place for confession (Canon 964, 2 and 3).

The whole rite of this *Form A* is composed of the following acts:

Rite of welcome. The priest kindly greets the penitent and welcomes him/her warmly. It is necessary to create a climate of confidence from the beginning without losing the religious sense of the act. The faithful, and if appropriate the priest also, start making the sign of the cross saying: "In the name of the Father and of the Son and of the Holy Spirit. Amen." Then the priest invites the person to put all his or her trust in God. The priest asks the Lord to grant the penitent knowledge of all sins, sincere repentance and the necessary grace to make a good confession to which the faithful must respond: *Amen.* Diverse formulae can be used for this initial prayer. It is also appropriate that both priest and penitent pray together asking for this grace and imploring God's mercy.

Proclamation of the Word. After this first contact, some text from the Scriptures is recited by heart or read, perhaps some brief sentence like: "God does not want the sinner's death, but God wants that person to turn from sinful ways and live" (cf. Ezk 18:23). "Let us, then, approach God with confidence as the giver of grace; we will obtain mercy and through God's favor, help in due time" (Heb 4:16). The Ritual in numbers 85-86 and 157-159 proposes a great variety of texts.

This proclamation of the Word is not frequently done in private confession, and this is understandable. Reading a biblical text slowly, in a prayerful and reflective atmosphere is something intrinsically valuable. Reciting some biblical verses, however, which the penitent hardly listens to, does not produce the desired fruit. God's Word is not magic: transforming a person's heart is not accomplished just by pronouncing a formula. God's Word demands the human cooperation and the necessary dispositions to produce fruit. Any speedy recitation of a text can hardly move hearts.

Confession of sins. After this preparation, there is the confession of sins. This should never be reduced to merely a *listing of faults*, for it must be an act of faith and of humble confession as an expression of the interior repentance. In some countries the penitents start by praying "I confess...," followed by the accusation of sins. At other times, especially for those who confess once a year, they merely say: "Help me, Father." The priest should also try to help those people who approach him with good will. It is preferable though that the penitent take the initiative. If the suggestions or the questions of the confessor are needed, there is the impression of the sacrament being an interrogation or an investigation into a person's private life; this impression should be avoided. It is better to suggest to the penitent the need for sincerity and a spontaneous accusation, and then to try to infuse confidence in God's mercy, repentance from all one's sins and a sincere intention to avoid them. The confessor may also guide penitents to especially fix their attention on the attitudes and situations of sin of their life instead of focusing on the Church's precepts: I have eaten meat on Friday, I did not attend mass on Sundays...

Satisfaction or penance. The accusation of sins is normally followed by a brief exhortation by the priest and any advice he considers appropriate. In any case, there is a clear need for the priest to be understanding, welcoming and kind. The refusal of sin cannot be seen to mean the priest's refusal to the repentant sinner. Many confessors have caused grave damage to penitents because of their lack of kindness and warmth. Popularly the work of *satisfaction* imposed by the priest is still called "penance". It is one of the most neglected segments in the present practice. The Rite of Penance recommends a brief dialogue on the satisfaction to be imposed. Generally it is not done nor it is worth doing, except in the case of frequent confessions and with persons willing to eliminate the roots of sin and to progress in their sanctification. The penitent's personal situation must always be taken into consideration: age, status, profession, whether a dedicated Christian or someone who receives the sacrament only once a year.

Prayer of the penitent.   The priest then invites the penitent to manifest sincere repentance through any prayer or through some other similar formula. The Rite proposes diverse samples (nos. 95-101). The traditional act of contrition "O my God, I am heartily sorry..." can be recommended. This is the moment to say it; definitely not during the absolution.

Imposition of hands and absolution.   To give the absolution, if the place is conducive, the priest stretches out his hands, or at least the right hand, over the penitent's head. Physical contact is not necessary, but it is a biblical gesture for consecration and blessing which needs to be restored. During the absolution, the faithful must attentively listen in silence to the word of pardon and answer "Amen" at the conclusion. The custom of making the act of contrition during the absolution needs to be abandoned.

Thanksgiving and farewell.   There should always be a word of thanksgiving to the Lord, "because God is good, because his merciful love is everlasting." A "well-made confession" is a liberating act that invites us to happiness and to thanksgiving. We must feel it and express it through some prayer or acclamation. The farewell words can be taken from the Rite: "Our God has forgiven your sins. Go in peace," but some other more familiar words can be added, according to the circumstances.

The question that any priest can ask regarding this brief exposition of the ritual is the following one: Is all this accomplished in the private confession of a penitent? We must answer in all honesty that ordinarily it is not. For this reason we said at the beginning that we have not yet taken advantage of many possibilities offered by the present *Ordo Paenitentiae*. I do not want to pinpoint here intolerable abuses, but one thing seems evident: all this ritual cannot be duly accomplished when there is a fixed schedule of confessions and other penitents waiting for their turn. This unsatisfactory reality will not stop us from perceiving the great positive values of this form of celebration.

Values of the Private Personal Reconciliation

No one disputes the fact that in order to correct the excessive individualism which for centuries has characterized the form of receiving the sacrament of penance, the Second Vatican Council insisted mainly on the social, ecclesial and community aspects. It believes that these should accompany its celebration and strongly recommends community celebration and the active participation of all the faithful.[1]

This does not hinder the acknowledgment that each celebration has its own value and its own purpose. To limit ourselves to only one form of celebration would be to impoverish the richness of the means of sanctification that the Church offers; while unintentionally but profoundly damaging the faithful. I personally believe that for the good of the many Christians who want and need it, the rite of reconciliation of a penitent alone cannot be abandoned and must continue existing in the Church but with possible improvements. This means of sanc-

---

[1] Cf. SC 27; 72; 109-110; LG 11.

tification that has helped so many persons throughout the Church's history cannot be denied nor made difficult for those still seeking it.

If any person needs further convincing of my appreciation and esteem for the private confession, expressed in writing and in word, let them read chapter IX of my book *"El Sacramento de la Reconciliación"* entitled *La confesión frecuente por devoción*, pages 301-315. I do not want to repeat the reasons for favoring the private confession given there and in other writings.

Today as yesterday this form of "confessing" is not *the only form nor the best form* for receiving the sacrament of penance. However, it is the only form many recommend because they have the tendency to reduce the whole celebration of the sacrament to the private confession. This is in open opposition to the Second Vatican Council's doctrine and continues to be a cause of great damage to the faithful.

When one reads of confession in the great eulogies from the Middle Ages and modern theologians, it should be remembered that they spoke of private confession. That was the only form of sacramental reconciliation known to them as evident in the anthological texts from Thomas Aquinas and Bonaventure through Martin Luther and Alphonsus of Liguori or Fr. Faber and Pius XII. All these factors must be taken into consideration in order not to reject or to despise a mode of receiving the sacrament and a means of sanctification during centuries of fruitful experience in the Church.

As the pope says in the exhortation *Reconciliation and Penance,* this form allows for greater value to be given to the most personal and essential aspects comprehended by the penitential forms. In the dialogue between the penitent and the confessor, the totality itself of the utilized elements (the biblical texts, the personal prayer, the form of "satisfaction" chosen, etc.) are components which make of this type of sacramental celebration the most adequate one for the concrete situation of the penitent (no. 32).

The functions exercised by the priest in his penitential ministry as judge, father, doctor and teacher are accomplished more thoroughly in the private reconciliation of a penitent alone. Like sin, if conversion is a personal act, it affects the most intimate aspects of a person. The manifestation of this conversion is in the intimate and the trusting dialogue with the priest. The stimulus that penitents can receive from the confessor to overcome situations of sin, plus the orientations regarding the plan to follow and the impulse to persevere on the road of virtue, are exceedingly significant values. They are more easily found in the peaceful and quiet individual confession of the first form than in the community celebration.

The individual confession has also the value as a *sign* of the encounter in the person of the minister between the sinner and the Church's mediation. This mediation of the Church is more clearly manifest in the other celebrations, though it is necessary to emphasize here that it is not absent in the private celebrations. In front of the confessor, the penitents acknowledge their sinfulness before God and before the Church and then confess their sins. This gesture is undoubtedly an authentic proof of their sincere conversion. "It is a liturgical gesture... deeply personal."[2]

For these major reasons, when sincerely carried out, individual reconciliation is a necessary and unique form for many persons and for diverse occasions. Hence this form cannot nor should it be abolished in the Church.

FORM B: RECONCILIATION OF SEVERAL PENITENTS WITH INDIVIDUAL CONFESSION AND ABSOLUTION

For two major reasons, this form of celebration is the most frequent among the communitarian forms:

---

[2] *Rec. et Paenit.,* no. 31.

1. Because under the present legislation, this form is the only sacramental form permitted as an ordinary mode.
2. Because the faithful who participate in a penitential celebration generally wish to receive the sacrament. They are less attracted by a non-sacramental penitential celebration of the Word.

This *Form B* is rather a synthesis of the other two forms: on the one hand penitents participate in the community character of the celebration in most of its elements (preparation, listening to the word, homily, examination, thanksgiving). On the other hand, this form personalizes two important aspects of the sacrament: the confession and the absolution. In the setting of Form B, personal dialogue and a more existential commitment are made possible.

In essence, it is a provisional, or transitory form, the *Form C* not yet being permitted as the ordinary mode: reconciliation of many penitents with general confession and absolution. *Form B* seems of little coherence liturgically: the community celebration is interrupted to give way to the individual acts. Later again it seems to be a community act of little relevance. Before the new Rite was published it was customary for all priests to give the absolution together, after the confessions. With this form, time was still available for a peaceful confession; and the absolution gained greater relevance. The Rite prescribes individual confession and absolution (*Rit.*, no. 28).

There are three main *inconveniences* of this form:

1. The interruption of the community celebration gives way to an individual action, precisely in two important moments of the sacrament — confession of sins and absolution.
2. The difficulty for many parishes to obtain a sufficient number of priests for this form of celebration. That these celebrations are usually held during significant liturgical seasons or on the main feastdays can partly compensate for this difficulty.

3. The imposed brevity in the accusation of sins and in the personal exhortation, especially when there are many penitents and only few confessors. It has always seemed a considerable inconvenience particularly for groups of youths to leave their seats for their brief confession and then return until the rest of the group finishes this stage. This gives the impression that what is essentially important is merely the repetition of sins to the confessor and the reception of absolution. The remainder of the celebration seems to be of secondary importance. Besides, on these occasions long confessions with consultations about situations in life, problems or doubts concerning personal conduct, or a long exhortation just cannot be permitted, because it would excessively prolong the celebration. For those waiting for the remainder to confess, these "delays" would cause restlessness and further distractions.

Though not included in the rite, because of these acknowledged inconveniences, in some places another legitimate form has spontaneously sprung up. In this form there is a common preparation — entrance song, greeting, prayer, biblical reading, homily, examination, act of contrition and prayers of the faithful. Following on from these, there is continuation as in the rite of reconciliation of one penitent alone. There is no waiting for the thanksgiving and a common dismissal because the individual confessions start according to the established order. The other penitents return to their assignments and then return to the center in small groups as the previous ones finish. This arrangement may be practical for large schools. But it would be better and more suitable if there were a common absolution and a conclusion comprising a thanksgiving and dismissal.

In order to avoid such inconvenience, it is preferable to arrange the community celebrations of *Form B* with small groups or with many confessors. In any case, it is preferable to impose a common satisfaction and after the confessions for all the priests to give absolution together. For the time being though we must maintain the norms of the Rite, which prescribe the individual absolution.

This celebration, besides focusing on small groups, is also useful for medium sized religious communities. Where the celebration takes only the necessary time, confessions can be made in a calm and peaceful atmosphere, even when there is only one priest. This form is really an introduction to the following form.

FORM C: RECONCILIATION OF MANY PENITENTS WITH GENERAL CONFESSION AND ABSOLUTION

This form was officially introduced in the new Rite as a new sacramental mode of receiving the sacrament of penance. Although unfortunately the present legislation has reduced it to extraordinary and exceptional cases, it is as valid, as legitimate and as effective as either of the other two. In the sixties especially after the Second Vatican Council, in many churches, above all in Holland and in Belgium, this *Form C* was practiced as the ordinary and regular mode once a month or once a week. At that time the New Rite of Penance, in which this form was foreseen as the ordinary one, took considerable time to be published. When this subject of confession was under discussion by the committee for the liturgical reform, the unexpected intervention of the Congregation for the Doctrine of the Faith cut short many hopes.

In the famous *Normae Pastorales* of 1972, just before the publication of the *Ordo Paenitentiae,* some restrictions were applied and the general absolutions were greatly limited. These changes had been considered as abusive and as the fruit of "some erroneous theories concerning the sacrament of penance."[3]

In itself the approval of this community celebration with a general confession and with a general absolution means a

---

[3] AAS 64 (1972) 510.

great step forward with regards to the old Rite. Conversely it also means a great step backward regarding what was already in practice and what was prepared by the first commission on the *Ordo Paenitentiae.*

Given this present situation, we now present *what this celebration consists of and under which conditions it may be practiced.* Pointing out its advantages and dangers, it is necessary to comment on the possibility and on the convenience of making this form of celebration the ordinary mode of receiving the sacrament.

Norms that at Present Regulate the Celebration of Form C

Let us start by saying that this form of celebration is not new in the Church. It was practiced in the ancient Church for centuries with remarkable variations according to circumstances.

In accordance with the norms given by the Congregation for the Doctrine of the Faith in 1972, the new Rite of Penance admits only *Form C* for extraordinary and grave cases of necessity.[4] In effect, while this greatly limits its practice, let no one conclude that the participant in such a celebration is less forgiven or half-reconciled. This form is fully efficacious as is any other form of the sacrament.

The norms which regulate the present celebration take for granted a dogmatic understanding which I consider false. Like the new Canon Law (cc. 960-964), the exhortation *Rec. et Paenit.* (nos. 32-33) and other documents of the Roman Curia or of the bishops' conferences, the following legislation tends to reduce the normal use of Form C instead of opening up and favoring the practice of this form of celebration.

This is also the result with the ordinances of the Spanish Bishops' Conference issued on November 1988 and approved

---

[4]Cf. *Rit.*, nos. 31-35, *Normae Pastorales*, AAS 64 (1972) 510-514.

by Rome, and in the *Pastoral Instruction* on the sacrament of penance, approved on April 1989.[5] The major thrust of the documents aims at avoiding abuses and warns about certain liberties that spring up from time to time due to pastoral convenience or sheer abuse. There is excessive fear that if *Form C* becomes the ordinary mode, many persons may totally abandon the individual confession and may limit themselves to the celebrations of a general confession.

In general, it is not possible to deny the negative impression caused by the reading of the norms (*Pastoral Norms*, Code of Canon Law, Norms of the Spanish Bishops' Conference, etc.). Instead of focusing on a worthy celebration of the sacrament of reconciliation they focus on the required conditions for receiving the general absolution. The important theological and pastoral aspects are relegated to the second position, thus giving a false impression. It may seem that what really matters is to determine whether it is licit or not to receive the general absolution in such or such conditions and whether the given norms are obeyed. This is a regrettable state of affairs.

The present norms regulating this celebration with a general confession and with a general absolution are found in the same ritual (nos. 31-33), in the Code of Canon Law (cc. 960-964) and in any manual on penance.[6] It is necessary here nevertheless to recall the essential factors.

General Principles

Only in cases of grave necessity may general absolution be administered without a previous individual confession. It is understood that there is a grave necessity:

---

[5] See the *Boletín oficial de la Conferencia Episcopal Española*, no. 22, April 5, 1989, pp. 59-60. *Dejáos reconciliar*. Instrucción pastoral sobre el sacramento de la penitencia, Madrid, 1989.

[6] Cf. D. FERNANDEZ: *El Sacramento de la reconciliación*, Valencia, 1977, pp. 294-296; D. BOROBIO: *Reconciliación penitencial*, Bilbao, 1988, pp. 203-205.

1. When there are not sufficient confessors to hear the confessions of each one in due time. For this reason and for a long time the faithful are involuntarily deprived of the sacramental grace of penance and of holy communion.

2. This may happen in mission fields, but also in other places due to the large numbers of faithful.

3. If there are sufficient confessors, the large number of faithful is still not a sufficient cause. These cases concerning numbers of faithful can be foreseen and an adequate number of priests must be secured in time in order to make it not necessary to give general absolution.

4. The bishops, after exchanging views with the other members of the bishops' conference, are to judge and to determine whether their own country meets the required conditions and circumstances for general absolution. In Spain, the Bishops' Conference has determined that ordinarily such conditions are not met.

On the part of the faithful

In this form, for the faithful to be able to receive general absolution, it is required:

1. That they have the correct disposition, that is, that they repent of their sins, that they be determined to change, that they be ready to atone for any related scandals and damages, etc. These dispositions are clear and are required for any private or community celebration.

2. That they be ready to individually confess in due time all grave sins not yet confessed.

3. Unless there is a just cause, the individual confession must be made before receiving the next general absolution. Canon 963 prescribes that it must be made at

least once a year, as imposed by the Church's general commandment. But this canon adds "that one must approach the individual confession *as soon as possible*, at the first opportunity." It is not necessary to repeat that this disposition seems to be unreasonable.

Norms for the priests

Priests are urged to warn the faithful, after the homily or within the Mass, that in order to receive general absolution they must be duly prepared, that is, repenting of their sins and having the intention to amend themselves and to atone for the damages or scandals that they might have caused.

That the faithful who have grave sins are obliged to confess them afterwards, in due time.

That there be imposed satisfaction to be fulfilled by all; to which the faithful could add another one, if they wanted (*Rit.*, no. 35a).

Finally, in order to express outwardly their wish to receive absolution, the priest (the deacon or another minister) will invite the faithful to make some visible sign to manifest their will and their disposition to receive absolution; perhaps to kneel, to bow down, or to come around the altar. After this, they will all recite together the general confession "I confess to almighty God...." Some other prayers could be added ending up with the Lord's Prayer. Absolution follows with the ample formula of the Rite, number 151.

Obviously, each and everyone of the norms cannot be expounded here. Some of them, though, do not seem suitable at all, while some others clearly must be considered for a worthy reception of the sacrament.

Present Problems

This *Form C* could be the most desirable mode for the Christian community to celebrate the sacrament of penance, were it to become one of the ordinary modes of reconciliation. This in fact is not the case:

1. Because it has been granted more as an exception than as a generally accepted form.

2. Because many limitations and difficulties have been made to hinder its celebration.

3. Rather than referring to the sacrament of penance, the present ordinances and exhortations refer to cases in which it is permitted to impart the general absolution and of the conditions required for receiving it.

4. The obligation is imposed on the faithful to confess privately afterwards all grave sins that could not be confessed in such a public rite.

5. This obligation creates unnecessary problems. For example, if persons after having received a general absolution do not fulfill the condition to confess privately to a priest all grave sins, do they commit a new sin? What is to be said concerning sins which were forgiven and from which they were absolved, if afterwards they did not fulfill the condition of the private confession. Do those sins come back to life?

These are hypothetical problems, which derive from an unsatisfactorily loose understanding of the celebration. It is simple to reply that penitents did not have the necessary dispositions because they lacked the will to confess afterwards and therefore their sins were not forgiven. It could also happen however that, in fact, they did then have the will, and only afterwards lost it. It is not difficult to hypothesize that some people understand that situation after having participated in a community celebration with a general absolution. They understand that they are already reconciled with God and with the Church. Therefore they do not need to fulfill any further requirement.

All these problems are false in the eyes of God. The precept to confess privately to a priest afterwards is a church precept and not a divine precept. The most desirable and most just approach would be to avoid creating any problem and guilt complex.

6. Since the evolution of the forms of penance has not finished, it is preferable to avoid pinpointing defects and difficulties in the present practice. It is far more preferable to underline the values and advantages of this particular form, in the hope that for many Christians some day it will be accepted as the ordinary means for healing and reconciling.

Values and Advantages of the Reconciliation of Several Penitents with a General Confession and a General Absolution

Aside from those indicated by the new Rite of Penance (nos. 22 and 77) and aside from others we have already presented in another book,[7] these need further emphasis:

1. Within the Christian community we have already indicated that liturgically this form seems the most complete, coherent and desirable mode to celebrate conversion and reconciliation. Here the recommendation of the Second Vatican Council is fulfilled: "It must be emphasized that rites which are meant to be celebrated in common, with the faithful present and actively participating, should as far as possible be celebrated in that way rather than by an individual and quasi-privately" (SC 27). In this Form C of celebration, the Church community intervenes in a more direct way with prayers, fraternal correction and mutual reconciliation. One of the aims pointed out by the council is more fully realized: "The rites and formulae of penance are to be

---

[7] D. FERNÁNDEZ: op. cit., pp. 296-298.

revised so that they more clearly express both the nature and effect of the sacrament" (SC, 72).

2. The Rite of Penance says in its number 8 that "the entire Church, as a priestly people, acts in different ways to carry out the task of reconciliation entrusted to her by God." This participation of the entire community is better achieved in community penitential celebrations in which all those gathered together listen to the word of God, intercede for one another, acknowledge their sinfulness before the entire community. They implore forgiveness from God and the community and then receive all together the happiness of being reconciled with God and with one another in the Church (cf. *Rit.*, no. 4).

3. This form also makes easier the renewal of the entire penitential process by spacing it in different phases:

    a. A day is devoted to the welcome, to biblical readings, to the homily and to the examination.

    b. Another day is dedicated to the deepening of repentance, of one's revision of life and the imposition of some works of satisfaction, as a proof and as a sign of a true conversion.

    c. Finally another day is fixed for the whole community to receive together sacramental reconciliation and to celebrate with happiness God's forgiveness in thanksgiving and gratitude.

    Proposed and desired by many for some occasions, this plan cannot become the general norm nor a frequent practice. Nor should it look either so utopian as to seem impossible to celebrate with groups of dedicated Christians, with retreat groups or in religious communities and basic Christian communities.

4. According to *Form C*, provided they always have the opportunity and full freedom for the individual confession,

this type of celebration is ideal for religious communities, for retreat groups and for any similar groups.

Just to give only one example, in religious communities, grave sins are unlikely to exist. Since there is no obligation to confess venial sins, the celebration can be held with a general confession. This practice can be followed within the present norms, and especially when members of the community spontaneously accuse themselves of their faults before God and before the community. Through this means every step is better placed and more suitable for it avoids the interruption of the community celebration with the individual confession.

5. Although any theological advantage is always of major concern, the practical advantage of this form of celebration is that it can be held with only one priest. In *Form B* if there are many penitents, many priests are needed in order not to excessively prolong the waiting time between the individual confession and the thanksgiving and dismissal. In this *Form C* there may be several priests as when concelebrating the holy eucharist, but only one of them is needed to organize and to preside over the entire celebration.

Dangers

There can be no denial that if *Form C* becomes the ordinary form, in spite of its many advantages, it would also contain potential problems.

The most significant danger is this: if these celebrations without an individual confession become ordinary, many persons would limit themselves to them and would totally abandon the private individual confession. For many persons, these celebrations would become the only mode of receiving the sacrament of penance.

I do not deny that danger, but exaggerations should be avoided. It is also true that over the centuries for Catholics, individual confession and absolution have been the only mode of sacramental reconciliation. "People used to confess during Mass" — and unfortunately this practice still continues — to the extent that the sacrament of penance has been reduced to a minimal expression. This practice evolved over centuries, and there has been no determined and clear intervention by the Church to improve the situation. Let us address this issue in parts:

a. In essence, many Christians do not go to confession any more, therefore the feared evil is already present and greater than the suspected evil. I believe that those who would come back to receive worthily the sacrament of penance would far outnumber those who would abandon the practice of private confession.

b. Most Christians who confess sometime in a lifetime or, at most, once a year to fulfill a precept and not because of any necessity or personal conviction concerning healing and reconciliation, tend to make their confession quite a mechanical and impersonal one. In fact nothing is lost with respect to Christian life even though persons refrain from confessing individually. For centuries there was no sacramental private confession nor the precept to confess once a year. Even so, there were still fervent Christians, saints, martyrs and legions of religious who never ever received the sacrament of penance. Those Christians who seldom confess and even then do so mechanically, can gain much and lose nothing. Provided that they participate in a well prepared community celebration: with biblical readings, exhortations, examination of conscience, prayers of the faithful, and the acknowledgment of one's sinfulness before the community, penitents fulfill all the requirements of a general confession. This procedure is more important and more desirable for conversion and the forgiveness of sins than any individual confessions that are made merely out of obligation: for example, being a member of a confraternity, on the occasion of a daughter's or a son's wedding (after ten or fifteen years without going to confession), on a daughter's or son's first communion, etc. To be realistic and open: those who participate in a well conducted community celebration with its general confession are far better disposed to the sacramental reconciliation than those persons who approach the confessional for a private confession under the above mentioned conditions. These celebrations do more to help the faithful in their Christian lives than the obligation of individual confession. This form actually does not fulfill the obligation, or fulfills it in a clearly inferior way. A practice of "celebration of penance with many penitents, and with a general confession and absolution" is far preferable to nothing, that is, to the practical disappearance of all forms of penitential celebrations.[8]

c. Private and personal confession is a need of the heart and as such is a great help and consolation for many people. It is a manifestation and sign of an authentic conversion. In order to re-orient some persons in difficult circumstances in life, it is sometimes necessary. If the individual reconciliation is so necessary in specific circumstances and so appreciated by the faithful, as affirmed by many recent documents, there is no need to fear that this practice may disappear. If it is abandoned by those who do not practice it properly and by those to whom it is just a torment, then nothing is lost. Those who approach the priest searching for spiritual help, grace and forgiveness will not abandon this support.

---

[8] D. BOROBIO: *Reconciliación penitencial*, Bilbao, 1988, p. 206.

Each form of celebration is designed to satisfy a specific need, so therefore none of them should supplant another. As the exhortation *Rec. et Paenit.* already warns, under the present legislation which considers *Form C* as extraordinary, exceptional use of the third form of celebration should never lead to a lower consideration and even less to the abandonment of the ordinary forms. Nor are we to consider this form as an alternative to the others" (no. 32). On the day in which this *Form C* becomes the ordinary one, both pastors and their faithful should choose those forms of celebrations deemed most fitting to their particular needs and situations. The perennial emphasis is to search always for the best for the faithful and for the Church.

Epilogue

The objective of this book is quite simple: to demonstrate the possibility of a form of penitential celebration which today is not accepted as the ordinary form of receiving the sacrament; and secondly, to eliminate the underlying error that has hindered the official acknowledgment of such a form.

What I affirm and defend in this book already has been written and taught by earlier theologians and scholars. I set out not to invent anything, nor do I teach anything new, but I do hope for the official acknowledgment of what is quite evident from history and from theology. Nowhere do I deny that problems concerning the sacrament of penance are not solved merely by introducing the general practice of general absolution without a previous individual confession. This community celebration constitutes a matter of faith, of sincere conversion, of conscience formation, and of due preparation. It also concerns a suitable time in which sinners can sincerely acknowledge their sins before God and before the community and can feel moved to atone for their sins and abandon them. This is a matter of feeling and living within the Church community, of the entire community, which is a mediator both of reconciliation and of forgiveness; and towards this goal catechetical formation and practice must aim. Precisely because many of those people most in need do not approach the sacrament of penance as it is presently structured, I believe that with God's grace, a well prepared community penitential celebration may be a decidedly more practical means to arrive at a sincere conversion. Together with reaching this goal is the deepening of one's own faith and the sharing of the happiness of reconciliation with the community. People prefer this form and attend these celebrations which give them peace, happiness and a sincere desire for a Christian life. During the summer of 1989 I was told of two practical cases where parishes in which this form of celebration was being practiced with much spiritual fruit. These celebrations will probably be stopped due to the complaints of other parish priests or to the ordinary's legitimate authority. This Form C could be the ordinary mode of celebrating the sacrament, but the present norms consider it as extraordinary; and the norms must be respected. The long history of the sacrament of penance with its innumerable changes, allows us to hope that someday the wishes and the spiritual needs of the people will be attended to by Church authorities. Those who believe that this aim is not important or that we are merely trying to elude the hardships of the private confession must seriously consider whether their attitude and the present norms are not hindering many people. So many people are prevented from receiving the sacramental grace with a much more thorough preparation than is made for an individual confession. So many people are deprived of the opportunity of entering into conversion and coming closer to the Church, because of the imposed restrictions and conditions which are not demanded by Christ himself.

On August 20, 1989 the pope addressed some 500,000 young people assembled at *Monte de Gozo* in *Santiago de Compostela:* "Truth is the deepest need of the human spirit. Above all you must be thirsty for the truth about God, about humanity, about life and about the world." But where is this truth? Who is this truth? Jesus Christ himself is the way, the truth and the life. If we have returned to Jesus Christ in order to find the sure way that leads to the truth, we must possess the Spirit of Jesus Christ, which will lead us to the plain truth. If we read the Gospel more often and allow ourselves to be permeated right through by its teaching and if we ponder its message in our hearts, like Mary, the Mother of Jesus (cf. Lk 2:19, 51), then many of the difficulties which we construct would simply disappear."

Allow me to finish with a story which illustrates my view. So often I have heard it applied to Buddhism, to the rabbis and to Christianity itself. Once upon a time several wise men were arguing about Buddha's doctrine. After many days of argument, and not being able to come to a consensus, Buddha decided to come to them and explain the true meaning of his words. But after listening to him reverently, the wise men answered him: "What is really important is not what you have taught, but the interpretation that the wise men have given your words. 'When Buddha dies, the schools are born'."[1] This simple story, certainly contains a profound lesson and responds to the truth of history. How many times we are directed to the interpretations of the theologians, of the Church, or of the magisterium instead of being directed to studying the very source! The Gospel of Jesus is simple and humane, far more than any human interpretation of it. To share my strong conviction concerning this particular aspect of Christian practice is essentially my sole object in presenting this study.

---

[1] Cf. ANTHONY DE MELLO, *The Prayer of the Frog*, Gujarat Sahitya Prakash, Anand, India 1988, p. 95.

PUBLICATIONS BY THE SAME AUTHOR ON THE SACRAMENT OF RECONCILIATION

Books:

Nuevas perspectivas sobre el sacramento de la penitencia. Edicep, Valencia 1971 (out of print).
El Sacramento de la Reconciliación. Edicep, Valencia 1977 (out of print).

Articles:

Renovación del Sacramento de la penitencia. Celebraciones comunitarias, "Pastoral Misionera," July-August 1967, pp. 45-59.
Renovación del Sacramento de la penitencia. Nuevas perspectivas, "Pastoral Misionera," September-October 1967, pp. 45-59.
Estructura interna del Sacramento de la penitencia, in "XXX Semana Española de Teología", Madrid 1972, pp. 473-488.
Futuro de la reconciliación sacramental en las comunidades religiosas, in "Vida Religiosa" 36 (1974) 405-416.
Valores y contravalores del Nuevo Ritual de la penitencia, in "Pastoral Misionera," March-April 1975, pp. 56-71.
Comunidad penitente, comunidad reconciliada, in "Vida Religiosa" 58 (1985) 375-381.